DOUBLE DUTY

DUAL IDENTITY

Raised in an Alcoholic/Dysfunctional Family and

CHEMICALLY DEPENDENT

by Claudia Black, M.S.W., Ph.D.

DOUBLE DUTY - Chemically Dependent - is excerpted from **DOUBLE DUTY**, Published in the United States by Ballantine Books, a division of Random House, Inc, New York and simultaneously in Canada by Random House of Canada Limited, Toronto.

For the purpose of anonymity, all names have been changed. Portions of stories have been altered to provide even further anonymity. Any resemblance to your life, or to the life of someone you know is coincidental and most likely due to the myriad of communalities in alcoholic and troubled families.

ISBN No.:0-910223-17-3

1st Printing, June 1990.

MAC PUBLISHING
a division of CLAUDJA, inc.
5005 East 39th Avenue
Denver, CO 80207
(303) 331-0148 • Fax (303) 331-0212

To my contributors, a.k.a.
Dennis, Lisa, Bob, Margaret and Bob

ACKNOWLEDGEMENTS

I would like to express my gratitude to all of the contributors who participated in this project. While only five life stories appear in the final book I am also greatly indebted to the others who offered stories. These people displayed not only a rare courage and generosity — they reached deeply into themselves and discovered yet another level of their own recovery.

I would also like to acknowledge my professional friends who gave me feedback on various chapters throughout this series. Leslie Drozd, Ph.D.; Victoria Danzig, M.S.W.; Don Steckdaub, M.A.; Doug Braun, M.F.C.; Jill Borman; Jael Greenleaf; Ed Ellis, Ph.D.; Dana Finnegan; Emily McNally; Mel Pohl, M.D.; Skip Sauvain, M.A.; Wynn Bloch, M.A.; Wayne Smith; Betty La Porte and Sam Ryan.

Thanks to Mary McClellan, of San Francisco who worked with me on the presentation of those stories; Barbara Shor, for her copy editing. Anne Marsin for her typing and retyping that was so vital in this project; Cheryl Woodruff, the editor of the Ballantine book Double Duty, from which this is edited; Jack Fahey, my husband and business partner who has read and reread every version of every chapter. He one more time walked me through this process every inch of the way.

CONTENTS

DOUBLE DUTY

While there has been a proliferation of books about Young and Adult Children of Alcoholics it is important to recognize that the Children of Alcoholics movement is still in its' infancy. We are only now beginning to understand the complexity of the trauma within the dysfunctional family systems so many Adult children have experienced and the ways this has compromised their adulthood.

Over the past few years thousands of Adult Children have begun their process of self-healing. There have been many wonderful miracles. Yet, as I watched people moving through their recovery, I have also seen many individuals hit a baffling impenetrable wall that halted their progress. There seemed to be a missing link or another piece to the puzzle. A very big piece of what I believe causes such blockage is the experience that I call **Double Duty.**

I define **Double Duty** as the intensified life experiences of ACOAs who have contended, not only with family alcoholism or dysfunction, but have also dealt with an additional set of circumstances that have profoundly affected their lives and their recovery. Many Adult Children belittle and criticize themselves for not moving through recovery as easily or as speedily as others they know. When ACOAs are unable to work through the recovery process with as much ease or speed as they would like, it is often because of their need to identify and address multiple issues in recovery. People who have multiple issues often have an additional need to protect themselves, and this may be why they do not connect with self-help groups or the therapy process as quickly as others.

One of the key premises of the ACOA recovery process is putting the past behind us. That only occurs when the truth of one's experience is acknowledged. Up to this time in the evolution of the ACOA movement, the stories told — and as a result the issues addressed — have tended to be very generalized. This stage of emphasizing the experiences all ACOA have in common has been incredibly valuable. However, now that many Adult Children have spent several years in recovery from their ACOA issues, I believe it is time to explore how Adult Children differ from each other. And that difference is what **Double Duty** is all about.

This book describes in detail the process the child experiences in an alcoholic family. It also examines the special problems of multiple issues — which I call **"Double Duty/Dual Identity"** (DD/DI) — that these Adult Children face and the step-by-step process of their recovery. We can no longer continue to apply generic recovery programs to all ACOAs. While general recovery information is most often what one needs to focus on in early recovery, in time an individual's unique life situation has to be and deserves to be addressed. By refusing to look at the specifics of an individual's experiences we can inadvertently trivialize the purpose of the entire movement.

The concept of **Double Duty** is not meant to encourage people to use their differentness to keep others away or to resist new opportunities. I believe we must first see our commonalities, and humble and comfort ourselves in the recognition that we are not unique. Although, we suffered separately, we have not suffered alone. Only after we have acknowledged this common ground should we undertake to explore what may have been unique in our experiences.

There are many reasons for differences among Adult Children. Birth order affects children differently, sex role expectations affect children differently. Who the chemically dependent parent is and the dynamics of how co-dependency shows itself create differences among ACOAs. Many areas merit exploration, but I have chosen certain areas that warrant deeper exploration for the Adult Child in the recovery process.

Double duty exists when a child has one major trauma-inducing dynamic in the family and there exists an additional dynamic that reinforces the consequences through added trauma or complexity.

For instance, if there is a terminally ill sibling in a child's family, growing up can be quite traumatic. But is does not have to create a lifelong trauma if there is a healthy family system to help the surviving child respond to the situation. However, put the set of circumstances in an alcoholic or otherwise troubled family, and the child involved will suffer many long-lasting effects from both issues. This is what I mean by a double duty situation.

In order to endure such trauma and added complexity — simply in order to survive — this child has to toughen up much more than other children. In adulthood, such survivors are likely to have their defenses much more rigidly in place and their emotions very hardened.

I envision the double duty COA as a small child, hunched over, dragging unwieldy boxes and overflowing bags of trauma, when suddenly a dump truck comes roaring up and adds another load of pain.

By contrast, **Dual Identity** is a special form of **Double Duty** in which one has at least two equally commanding aspects to one's identity — such as being a COA and a person of color or being a COA and gay or lesbian. It is like looking into a two-sided mirror and seeing one image of yourself on one side and an equally real but different image on the other side. Although the images are different, they are invisibly enmeshed. This leaves Adult Children even more confused about who they are and what is most important in their lives.

For the purpose of Adult Child recovery it is important to recognize that as an ACOA, there may be other, equally significant aspects of your identity that need to be recognized and addressed — beyond those of having been raised in a chemically dependent family — in order to experience a full recovery.

Double Duty/Dual Identity are examples of the synergistic effect of multiple-core issues that many Adult Children experience. The added dynamics of **Double Duty/Dual Identity** often force children to protect themselves even further. As a result, issues such as not trusting, not feeling, fear of losing control, and an overwhelming sense of shame are experienced even more deeply. It then becomes much more difficult for the afflicted ACOA to ask for help or to feel any hope. Very often the feeling of being overwhelmed by emotion or of having frozen emotions greatly impedes the ability to connect with a recovery process.

There are many people who know they are Adult Children, who know resources are available, who may even truly want to change their lives — yet always find that something seems to get in the way when they try to connect with a helping resource or try to stay involved once they've found that resource. There are others who are so powerfully defended against their pain that their level of denial is too strong for them even to recognize that their lives could be better. Still others become stuck in the process of recovery and "spin their wheels." These are often the DD/DI people. In this book we will explore the phenomena of being raised in an alcoholic/dysfunctional family and being chemically dependent.

"My father died from his alcoholism. Today, the difference between my father and me is that he died from his and I do not have to die from mine."

Adult Child

CHEMICAL DEPENDENT — DUAL IDENTITY

When you are raised in a chemically dependent home, alcohol and drugs become a central fixture in your life. Alcoholism and other addictions become a norm that is rarely, if ever, questioned.

Some COAs' earliest memories of play are creating their own bars and playing *"barmaid"* or *"bartender"* or playing *"spin me around so I can be drunk, too."* Alcohol has already become a tremendous force in their lives. It has the power to make their lives miserable. It has the power to render their parents out of control. These kids see their parents use alcohol and other drugs to successfully escape their feelings, responsibilities, and pain. By the time children from alcoholic homes reach adolescence — and sometimes even before — they may begin to emulate their alcoholic parents' behavior by turning to alcohol to erase their pain.

Alcohol and other drugs, such as marijuana, speed, cocaine, ice, crack, Librium or Valium, offer children an escape from a life full of powerlessness, loneliness, and fear; they medicate, they anesthetize. These mind-changing chemicals offer children a way to feel connected with others. In the Adult Child, they reduce the sense of isolation, offering a way of fitting into the crowd. This is a powerful countereffect to the *"alone in the crowd"* syndrome so characteristic of children of alcoholic homes. Alcohol and drugs offer a way for COAs to have fun. They can give the user a sense of power. The alcohol/drug abuse may even be a child's way of relating to the alcoholic parent on the adult's own terms. Many Adult Children who become chemically dependent as youngsters say that their drinking and using gave them something in common with their parents for the first time.

Every child who was aware that alcohol was inflicting a terrible wound on the family has said, *"It will never happen to me!"* And meant it. They boast defiantly that they will make sure they don't end up as their "old man" did, or they make a powerful statement not to repeat what happened in their lives because of their mother's drinking. They believed that they would have the willpower, the self-control, and the knowledge to be different. They believe some miracle will free them from the gut-wrenching fear born out of their family experience.

The problem is, becoming chemically dependent has nothing to do with willpower, self-control or knowledge. If it did, I believe that children from chemically dependent homes would be the least likely to become chemically addicted. Yet these addictions do repeat themselves within families.

The phenomenon becomes understandable when you observe the modeling these children have had for drinking and using chemicals. It is also obvious that alcohol and other drugs provide a relief and an escape from a very painful life. Moreover, there is evidence that strongly supports the physiological tendency toward chemical dependency when one is the child of an alcoholic.

Physiological Predisposition Toward Alcoholism

Children of Alcoholics are significantly more prone to chemical dependency than any other group of people. Research has shown that sons of alcoholics are five times more likely to become chemically dependent and daughters of alcoholics are two times as likely to become chemically dependent than individuals not raised in alcoholic homes.[(1)] It is estimated that as many as 60 percent of the adults and 75 percent of the teenagers in chemical dependency treatment programs come from alcoholic homes.

More and more research is beginning to show that this greater likelihood of chemical dependency is due, in part, to genetic factors. Research compared the incidence of alcoholism between twins. Such as the Veterans Administration study has supported a genetic predisposition to alcohol. In this research identical twins were not only more likely to share the disease of alcoholism than fraternal twins, but they also manifested more organic symptoms of the disease, such as alcoholic cirrhosis and psychosis.[(2)]

Adoption research confirms this genetic predisposition as well. Sons of alcoholics were four times more likely to become alcoholic than sons of nonalcoholics, regardless of whether they were raised by their alcoholic biological parents or by nonalcoholic adoptive parents. Adopted sons reared by nondrinking parents were just as likely to become alcoholic as sons reared by alcoholic biological parents. By contrast, sons of nonalcoholic biological parents, adopted by alcoholic parents, did not become alcoholic at an unusually high rate. Adopted daughters with alcoholic biological mothers were three times more likely to become alcoholic than other women, even when reared from an early age by nondrinking parents.[(3)]

Metabolic research has revealed that Children of Alcoholics, ranging in age from eight to thirteen, had lower zinc levels than children of nonalcoholic parents.[(4)] This finding suggests that before any alcohol ingestion, Children of Alcoholics have the same zinc deficiency that manifests itself in the chronic adult alcoholic population. Zinc deficiency has been associated with cerebellar dysfunction, learning disabilities, and schizophrenia. These findings suggest that school-age children may already be physiologically prone to alcoholism, and they support other research pointing to abnormalities in alcohol metabolism in Adult Children of Alcoholics.[(5)]

Schuckit's research indicates that it takes more alcohol for sons of alcoholics to become inebriated, but they have less ability to detect its effects than their peers, which sets them up for a higher level of intoxication before they identify being under the influence.[(6)]

In general, chemical dependency is linked directly to a physiological change in tolerance to alcohol or other drugs. It is accompanied by a psychological dependence characterized by personality changes, rationalization, denial, loss of control, and manipulation of the environment to make alcohol and drugs more accessible.

The progression is insidious. It demoralizes social interaction as well as physical and emotional well-being. It destroys the spirit. Once a person has crossed the line from social drinking to dependency, there is no going back. Recovery lies in breaking the pattern of denial and in seeking help that will support a life free from the ingestion of all mind-changing chemicals.

The Progressiveness Of Chemical Dependency

By the time Children of Alcoholics become adults, many already have several years of drinking and using behind them, and they have passed over the line into their own dependency. Others are only beginning to drink. Either way, a COA generally moves through the progression of chemical dependency much more quickly than the child of a nonalcoholic.

Children of Alcoholics may, in fact, find themselves in *"middle stage"* chemical dependency from the start. Others will start drinking in the early stage and gradually move through all the other stages of dependency. The younger a person is when they start drinking, the faster they will move through the stages. Females tend to progress through the stages of addiction more rapidly than males. A young female COA may never have a single day of *"normal drinking."* With all of these variables in play, the progression of the disease may be very rapid indeed. (See appendix for progression chart)

Dual Identity

When people are not only addicted, but have been raised in an alcoholic/addicted family, they have two identities. They are, first of all, chemically dependent; second, they are Adult Children of Alcoholics. Both issues will need to be addressed in their treatment and recovery.

Whether one issue needs to be addressed first or whether both need to be dealt with simultaneously depends on a variety of factors. Some chemically dependent people find that Adult Child issues affect the quality of their sobriety. Others discover that Adult Child issues set them up for relapse. Still others must address their Adult Child issues before they can recognize their own chemical dependency.

Sobriety First

It is my professional opinion that if people are alcohol/or drug addicted, they need to be clean and sober before they can adequately address Adult Child issues.

It is a monumental task simply learning how to get clean and sober and stay clean and sober. Historically, the Twelve Step self-help groups — which have had the most success in helping people accomplish that task — have found there is little room for ambiguity in the early months. I strongly agree. Generally speaking I believe that abstinence needs to be in place before other issues in recovery can be addressed. Only after some sober time has been achieved do we have the opportunity and the resources to look at underlying problems.

In those first few months we've typically focused on how not to use or drink and how to allow others to become a part of that process. We're learning how to listen to others who have gained abstinence and sobriety and how to follow their direction. We're busy putting the practical aspects of daily life back in order. This period of embryonic sobriety is not usually the best time for us to confront and challenge *"family of origin"* issues. Working on both issues simultaneously is too fragmenting. Very often we lose sight of the priority to not drink and use, and we will relapse.

Most individuals need to focus on recovery from addiction for as long as one to three years before they are emotionally, socially, and mentally prepared to begin another significant phase of the recovery process.

After at least three years sobriety, there is usually little to prevent us from addressing the way Adult Child issues might be interfering in our lives.

Even when chemically dependent people make major changes in their lives and are grateful for their sobriety, they often find that the quality of their sobriety may be hampered by their Adult Child issues, even though they are working through a Twelve Step program. For example, addicted people are often accused of being on a *"dry drunk."* This is a phrase used to describe a chemically dependent person who is physically clean and sober but lacking an emotional recovery process. Although they abstain from alcohol and drugs, their negative attitudes and often their behavior have not changed. In actuality they are displaying Adult Child symptoms such as rigidity, inability to trust, or the need to be in control.

Unfortunately any combination of Adult Child traits may contribute to eating disorders or compulsive behaviors such as workaholism or compulsive spending. They may also lead to inappropriate sexual behavior, sexual addictions, or extramarital affairs. Any or all of these hamper the development of healthy personal relationships and increase the likelihood that they will be distant and possibly even abusive. Nonrecovering Adult Children are more likely to experience depression, feel loneliness, and possibly even have thoughts of suicide — or actually commit suicide. This is a rough way to live sober. People deserve more, and more is possible. Addressing both identities — alcoholic and Adult Child — is often the key to a sustained and happy recovery.

Preventing Relapse

Many addicted Adult Children need to address specific Adult Child issues as they are getting sober in order to prevent a relapse. Adult Child issues could interfere with their ability to get and to stay clean and sober.

Often these relapse-prone issues are shame-based. For example, incest survivors frequently need to do some initial work around the molestation to develop enough belief in their worth to get sober. Sometimes rage, which is often based on people's profound feelings of inadequacy, will interfere with the ability to listen and follow directions long enough to become or stay sober. Many chemically dependent people must have an opportunity to address their shame, grief, and loss before they have the strength even to believe that they deserve to be sober. Such people usually need to be guided by a helping professional who is a chemical dependency specialist, knowledgeable about addictions and Adult Child issues.

The following relapse markers should help determine which Adult Child issues may need to be addressed up front to aid one's efforts toward sobriety and to help prevent a relapse.

Relapse Markers

Rigidity, Inflexibility:
- Inability to accept direction.
- The need to be right.
- Only seeing options in an all-or-nothing perception.

Inability to Ask for Help:
- Being saddled with the inherent feeling that all tasks are your responsibility.
- No faith in others.
- Asking for assistance being perceived as a sign of weakness.
- Not asking for assistance out of fear.

Inability to trust:
- Rigid self-reliance.
- Inability to let go.
- Inability to achieve closeness.

Desire for Excitement:
- Living life steeped in crisis.

• Without crisis, life is perceived as empty, boring.

Inability to Identify Needs:

• So busy responding to others' needs and wants, unable to focus on self.

• Low self-esteem, resulting in an inability to value and respond to personal needs.

Not Seeing a Crisis Until It Is a Problem:

• Inability to recognize cues and signal of a problem until it reaches crisis proportions.

• Denial, minimizing realities.

The Need to Look Good:

• By presenting one's physical self in a positive manner, one can hide the more vulnerable self.

• Distancing oneself from others to hide vulnerability.

Need To Be Perfect:

• A mask to cover shame.

• A way to look good.

• A manifestation of needing to be in control.

Control:

• The manipulation of people, places, and things in order to feel safe.

• The minimization and repression of feelings or withholding of feelings to feel safe.

• Compassion for feelings of inadequacy.

Shame:

• The belief that one is inadequate, defective, worthless.

• The belief that one is not capable, that one has inherent, irreparable faults.

Fixing Others:
• Focusing on others in an attempt to avoid focusing on self.
• Focusing on others to feel more powerful.

Inability to Identify Feelings:
• Not able to recognize feelings, therefore missing inner cues and signals to personal needs.
• Fear of losing control.
• Fear of exposing one's shame.

Enduring Intolerable Situations:
• Tolerating inappropriate situations; setting oneself up for victimization.
• Allowing others to be intrusive at one's expense.
• Being disrespectful of self.

Being Intrusive:
• Being disrespectful of others.
• Violating others' boundaries.

Wanting to Do Recovery by Oneself:
• Not being able to trust.
• Need to look good.
• Need to control.

All of the above issues have the ability to affect the quality of one's sobriety. In addition, not addressing them can prime a chemically dependent person for a relapse. In the past, when a recovering alcoholic demonstrated these markers, he or she used to be labeled as being on a dry drunk, when in fact such attitudes and behaviors may have resulted from being an Adult Child.

Adult Child Issues First

Many addicted people don't recognize the need to get sober until after they begin their Adult Child work. It is in addressing their Adult Child issues that they first begin to look at and identify their alcohol or drug addiction. For some people, it is simply safer to begin recovery with Adult Child issues; yet how much they do in recovery will be limited until they are clean and sober. Others simply cannot recognize their own addiction or believe in themselves enough to get help until they have lessened their denial and shame with Adult Child work.

Addicted people who begin ACOA recovery first may or may not find it necessary to postpone further Adult Child work to focus on their chemical dependency issues. If they are at a very early stage in their addiction, they may be able to work both programs simultaneously. However, if they are more middle-or late-stage addicted to alcohol or other drugs — particularly if inpatient treatment is necessary — then it is usually best to delay involvement in an ACOA program and concentrate on a program of abstinence.

The key approach for the people attempting to work through both recoveries simultaneously it to allow themselves to develop the support of other recovering alcoholic/addicts. Such support is critical to recovery and abstinence. Interacting with clean and sober recovering alcoholic/addicts offers vital direction.

LIFE STORIES

The following are stories of five Adult Children who are chemically dependent. Their recovery period ranges from three to ten years of sobriety. If you identify with their addictive process as you read their stories, be open to how alcohol and drugs may be influencing your life. See the appendix for further self-assessments. To have become chemically dependent is not a sign of weakness. It is not bad. It is simply a fact that warrants your immediate attention.

These five people will talk about their childhood, the impact of alcohol on their lives, their recovery, and how their Adult Child issues have come to play a significant role in their recovery process. Although these five people identify with the more hidden consequences, ultimately their addiction overrode their ability to hide or look good.

Growing-up Years

DENNIS

Age: 32
Mother: Alcoholic
Father: Alcoholic
Raised: Northern California
Socioeconomic Status: Working Class

Dennis' recovery from Adult Child issues is one of the more common alcoholic stories. He had been sober many years before he began his Adult Child recovery. In fact, he became sober before there were Adult Child resources. Over the years of his long-term sobriety, Dennis had allowed himself to develop a level of honesty that has been difficult for many. Because of this painstaking honesty, Dennis was able to admit that he was still very lonely and frightened. He felt something was missing in his recovery and sought out an Adult Child recovery program.

Dennis grew up in a large alcoholic family. He was the oldest of seven, and he remembers his childhood as being filled with chaos. Both his parents are alcoholics, and his family has had a history of alcoholism and addictive/compulsive behavior. Dennis' grandmother died of alcoholism; his younger brother is a recovering alcoholic; his sister and another brother are both compulsive overeaters; another brother is both an overeater and compulsive gambler; and his two remaining brothers are active alcoholics.

Dennis' father's drinking was always the primary issue in his family's relationship. Although his mother is also an alcoholic, Dennis' father was the more dominant figure in the household.

DENNIS:

"I can remember being Dad's favorite when I was really young, but about the time I was six or seven, that shifted. Suddenly Dad wasn't around anymore. He became a workaholic. When he was around, the only attention I got was negative. He was either telling us what to do or getting angry with us. He would become abusive and whip us with his belt. He was always sarcastic and would never give us a straight message. He seldom hugged us or showed any love."

Dennis internalized the pain he felt over this lack of love and attention. He felt unhappy and abandoned; he wasn't able to express this verbally, although these feelings did play themselves out in his dreams.

"I had nightmares a lot. One dream I used to have was that I was looking for my mom in a department store. Finally I saw her driving down the road. She was gone. She had left me all alone. I still have this dream as an adult.

"I wet my bed until I was seven, and I used to suck my finger at night. I thought I was bad for doing these things. I remember waking up in the morning feeling, I'm bad."

Many young children wet the bed through their grade-school years. While there are many theories about the cause of enuresis, pediatricians support the theory that stress is often the primary source of this behavior.

Dennis wasn't a bad child, but no one told him that. His thumb sucking and bed wetting were actually indicators of his need for greater nurturance and security.

Dennis remembers his family life being chaotic.

"There were lots of kids around, but none of us were very connected with each other. When I was younger no one ever stuck up for me. No one really ever paid attention to me. I could do what I wanted. My mom was always home. She always had dinner for us. It was just that I always felt lost in the house. She never seemed to have much time for us. In spite of this I never really thought about anything being wrong in our house."

Dennis was confused by the turmoil of living in a large family, and he was confused by the alcoholism. Neither he nor anyone else perceived alcoholism as a problem. The children grew up accepting chaos, unpredictability, mixed messages, and negativity as the norm.

Dennis went to Catholic school until he was in eighth grade, and for the most part he was a good student. His doing well in school was an effort to get approval and stay out of trouble. Yet he was not able to feel much personal satisfaction.

"I did well in school. I was an overachiever — I achieved for everyone else but me. I didn't do as well in sixth, seventh, and eighth grades because of peer pressure to be cool. But by ninth grade the pressure was more on me to succeed. I found out that if I did okay in school, I didn't get in as much trouble from my parents or teachers. I think in a way it was a matter of 'I'll be so good you'll be sorry for treating me poorly.'"

In spite of his determination to do well in school, most of Dennis' childhood and adolescence is foggy to him. This is because, after taking his first drink at thirteen, he fell into a pattern of heavy alcohol and drug usage.

LISA

Age: 42
Mother: Alcoholic
Father: Alcoholic: died when she was seven
Birth Order: Twin, one of four sisters
Raised: Wisconsin
Socioeconmic Status: Working Class

Lisa is similar to many Adult Children of Alcoholics in that the progression of her alcoholism moved quickly. Her drinking career spanned ten years, beginning in her late twenties. She got sober in her late thirties, and barely two years later a traumatic event led her to address Adult Child issues.

When Lisa was seven her father died in an airplane crash. Lisa's memories of her father are vague, but she does remember his drinking being a significant part of family life.

Lisa's mother was also alcoholic. Lisa said she didn't know alcohol was the cause of the problems in the home; she and her sisters thought her mother was just crazy. Excessive drinking was the norm. Lisa remembers her mother drinking and using tranquilizers on alternate days. She says yelling took place with the drinking, and nonverbal hostility emerged on the nondrinking days.

LISA:

"My mother and I were never close. After my father passed away, her drinking changed from going to the bar periodically to drinking in the daytime. I could depend on her to be drinking every day when I came home from school. She would usually start about three-thirty in the afternoon and drink until ten or eleven at night. It seemed as if

I was always fixing her a drink, or my sisters and I would take turns fixing her a drink."

Pouring drinks for a parent is often the only or the best way to have a relationship with the alcoholic parent. It may be the only time they approve of you — the only time they notice you without saying hurtful things. Often the only attention Lisa could get from her mother was inappropriate and embarrassing.

"Mom was always asking me to sing for her when her friends came to visit. She would call me into the kitchen and tell me to join in or sing a favorite song for her. I was embarrassed, but I still liked the attention I was getting from her, so I would do it. I knew this would please her, which is what I was always trying to do."

Pouring drinks was a way for Lisa to be noticed. Singing for her mother, in spite of the embarrassment, was another way. Wanting approval so much that you do things that are painful to you leads children to be hurt by others most of the time. Lisa was a prime candidate for victimization.

"I began to hate coming home from school because I knew it was always going to be the same old thing. My mother would single me out and yell at me. Then my sisters would tell me that I was just imagining that Mom didn't like me, that I was being too sensitive and overreacting. I would believe them and just keep trying to please Mom. I always wondered what was wrong with me because nothing I did ever seemed to be okay to Mom."

"No matter what you do, it's never good enough." This devastating attitude makes children try to be perfect. As a result they fail or give up and never try. Either way they never experience accomplishment. The problem with seeking approval in an alcoholic family is that what works one moment won't work the next — this is the fundamental unpredictability associated with alcoholic behavior.

One of four girls, Lisa was a loner and very shy as a child. She did spend some time with her twin sister, Laney, who was more outgoing.

"I always wanted to be a part of everything Laney did. She was my best friend as well as my sister. I could always turn to her for help, protection, and advice. Sometimes I would have girlfriends, but never more than one at a time. I just preferred to be alone and on my own. I never felt close to my other two sisters. Laney got along with both of them. But if I tried to get close to them, I felt as if I didn't belong. I always felt like I did things wrong and they didn't like me. It was easier just to stay by myself.

"The only person who ever believed me was Laney. Mom was always depressed or had something wrong with her. And if I tried to talk about it to my sisters, they would agree that she was crazy. They said that that was just the way Mom was. That was all there was to it. We never made any connection between her behavior and her drinking."

Lisa's close relationship with her twin is classic twin behavior. Twins often form a tight bond and a very private bond that creates greater isolation from others. Compensating for the lonliness in a troubled family, that bond can become even tighter.

It's common for children not to recognize a parent's true condition — to believe the parent is crazy rather than alcoholic. They may not identify it because 1) they don't have enough information; 2) they don't see the kind of drunkenness that is so often associated with alcoholism; 3) they don't see the drinking; or 4) they would feel greater helplessness by believing Mom to be alcoholic rather than crazy.

Lisa never knew what to expect from her mother. Often her mother would abuse the children verbally, accusing them of things they hadn't done.

"My mother became belligerent when she drank. Sometimes Laney would take the blame for something I was supposed to have done, when neither of us was at fault. Mom would always find something to be angry about. Laney could always talk her out of her anger, but if I tried to do this, it only made matters worse.

"Mom would never believe me, or she wouldn't listen. She would verbally harass me for days. Many times she would say, 'You hurt the ones you love the most.' She had me convinced that she loved me so much that that was why she was always punishing me. I would think, 'She really does love me. She doesn't hate me.' I grew up feeling and believing I was the crazy one, the bad one. I was a loner who was confused and didn't trust myself or anyone else. My goal was to stay out of the house."

When she was a teenager, Lisa began dating a boy she felt really understood her and how she felt. The boy had a twin brother who began dating Laney. Things seemed to be going well until, at fifteen, Lisa became pregnant.

"Once again, my mother was angry with me. At least this time I felt she had a reason. I felt very guilty for getting pregnant. I went to a home for unwed mothers and had planned to give up my child for adoption. This plan soon changed, however. When my mother was drunk she begged me to keep my son. I remember telling her, 'For you I will, Mom.' Inside, I felt as if I really should give him up. I wanted him to have a proper home with two parents, but I felt guilty, so I brought him home."

Lisa's profound need to please, her need for her mother's approval, was so great that it prevented Lisa from making a decision out of choice. She made a decision out of the need to please her mother. In her need to get approval, Lisa had never learned to make decisions on her own.

"Once the baby was home with us, my mother started saying that I was too young to be a mother and she wasn't going to be responsible for raising another child. She said she had already done her share. I was working full-time and going to school, but I let her know she wouldn't be doing anything at all, that he was my son and my responsibility. I'd really started to hate her by that point. I let her know I would raise my son without her help or support. I felt betrayed, confused, hurt and angry."

When Lisa was eighteen she and her baby's father got married. He had been in and out of jail before they married, and once they set up a home together, Lisa realized that he, too, was an alcoholic. The marriage lasted for ten years, during which time Lisa had two more sons and a daughter.

"I didn't have the foggiest idea how to be a mother or a wife. I'd had four children by the time I was twenty-three. I stayed in that marriage until I couldn't stand it any longer. I thought I'd lose my mind before it was over. I left the marriage at age twenty-eight, again feeling very angry, hurt, and confused. I just kept asking myself what I'd done wrong.

"I always felt as if I must have done something wrong to keep the marriage from working. I wasn't drinking at the time, but I didn't know about AA or Al-Anon. I just know that the marriage's failure must have been my fault in some way."

The script for Lisa was clear. She was always at fault. She must do better. Hurt, anger, and confusion followed her from her mother's home into the years of marriage. Lisa never had the ability to try life on her terms until age twenty-eight.

BOB

Age: 37
Mother: Co-dependent
Father: Alcoholic
Birth Order: Oldest of two
Raised: Northwest
Socioeconomic Status: Upper middle class

Bob's story depicts the life of an Adult Child who drank abnormally from the first day he began to drink. Although he became dependent on alcohol at a young age, Bob was nevertheless functional.

He was able to earn a law degree and begin a successful practice before his disease overcame him.

When Bob was a child, alcoholic drinking was the norm. Alcohol was so central to his family, it infiltrated every aspect of his life, even his play time.

BOB:

"I remember one time when I was a kid we had a washing machine delivered to the house, and my parents let me keep the large packing case to play with. I decided to make a bar out of it and put a board on the back of the box to hold the bottles I'd fished out of the garbage to serve my imaginary patrons. I was only about six or seven at the time.

"I know that my father drank and that I didn't like it, but no one was there to tell me what alcoholism was. It was as if we were supposed to be a happy family, but there was always this unacknowledged problem — his alcoholism. It was there, and I was too, sort of like going to a picnic where it rained a lot.

"Financially we were okay. Emotionally, though, it was as if my father was frozen in a huge block of ice. I think he tried to be close to us when we were kids. He just wasn't very successful. He was always embarrassed by positive emotions unless he was drinking. I grew sick, however, of the emotions he expressed when he was drinking. They weren't real for me, somehow. I didn't believe them. I supposed I just grew to distrust anything that came out of his mouth while he was drinking."

Bob's father made an effort to spend time with Bob, but their times together were usually marred by his father's drinking behavior.

"I remember his being a Boy Scout leader and our going on camp outs and canoe trips, but it wasn't really 'good' time I spent with my father. Even though we were both there, he was always in charge. He couldn't listen to others. Life was his way. There was no flexibility. He was so rigid. There was no fun.

"We would go on trips as a family, but what I remember the most about them were bad incidents involving my father's drinking. His

drinking would frighten me. I would hear him at night bouncing off the walls on the way to the bathroom. He was overweight and usually naked, and the whole thing was disgusting. Sometimes when he drank early he would fall asleep; then he would wake up and prowl the house in the middle of the night.

"Mostly I have this image of my dad sitting in front of the television, drinking. I never felt he had any interest in me.

"I felt lots of love during my childhood from my mom and relatives, but really very little from my father. I remember Dad's constant need to be supported, reassured, and told that he was a good father. He would elicit these responses by telling us that he was not appreciated, that nobody knew how hard it was for him, that nobody really appreciated him, and that all he was good for was money. All the while he was about as accessible as a prickly cactus. He wanted us close, but he dodged us when we approached. Emotionally, as far as my father's love was concerned, we were living on bread and water."

Bob did have some support from his mother and other family members. Even so, the support of others cannot completely compensate for the wounding of a child by the alcoholic parent.

"I felt as if my mother was very available to us when we were growing up. She didn't work outside the home, and I have a warm feeling about her being there. To be sure, we never discussed Dad's drinking, but she was dependable, caring, and loving. I also had a very warm relationship with my maternal grandmother. Mom used to visit my grandparents for coffee almost every day, and I remember playing in their house, eating Grandma's cookies and cakes. Theirs was an open, loving family, and I loved to go there. I also had a special aunt and uncle who had no children of their own. They lived near us, and I often stopped to visit them on my way home from school."

Bob said that high school was a slow start for him, but *"a strong finish."*

"I felt awkward, unattractive. There was the 'in group,' the athletes and the cheerleaders, and then there was the other group. I was

in the other group. However, this was the academically superior group, and I got a lot of satisfaction from being a part of it. I had at least found something I could do well."

Bob also had a significant relationship during his teenage years. He said it was not a sexual relationship, but one that was important to him.

"She made me feel good — maybe just by paying attention to me. It gave me someone to talk to, though we didn't talk about family things. But I could talk about other things — like my classes, and what I wanted to do later."

Bob went on to college emotionally numbed and without much thought about his growing up years.

MARGARET

Age: 35
Mother: Alcoholic
Father: Alcoholic, sober her growing-up years
Birth Order: Youngest of four
Raised: Maryland
Socioeconomic Status: Working class

Margaret's story is an example of an alcoholic whose Adult Child issues interfere with her ability to do what she needs to do to maintain sobriety. She must work on her Adult Child issues to prevent relapse.

Although both her parents were alcoholics, Margaret's father became sober three years before she was born. Her father recently died at the age of eighty-nine. He was thirty-eight years sober in Alcoholics Anonymous. Margaret's mother began to drink when Margaret was three years old. Margaret is certain that her mother is an alcoholic. She remembers her drinking constantly, the slurring of words, the many fights between her parents. Basically she describes her mother as being *"not available."*

Margaret's dad was considerably older than her mom and was retired when Margaret was born. Her mother had been a maid in a hotel. Margaret remembers little of her childhood and describes her early years as vague.

MARGARET:

"My childhood was slow, a nothingness. My mom was real unavailable, and Dad was only accessible after he came home from an AA meeting. That's when I could approach him with my homework and he would help me. He was always in a better mood then."

Margaret's association of her father's involvement in Alcoholics Anonymous was positive, as his return from meetings was a positive time. Yet Margaret was in an unusual position in that her father, who was actively involved in a recovery program for his alcoholism, was married to a practicing alcoholic. In spite of Margaret's father's recovery from addiction, Margaret's family was still a highly dysfunctional family unit.

What Margaret remembers most is the constant fighting between her parents and cruelty on the part of her brother and oldest sister. Margaret says that the kids basically raised themselves.

"My brother and my oldest sister were much older than I was. My youngest sister was only three years older, but we weren't close. My brother lived with us until he finished high school and joined the service. I used to dread it when he came home, and as a defense, I would always get sick. He used to tell me that I was always so bad. And he and my sister used to have to lock me in the closet.

"I remember having lots of nightmares as a child. I would dream that our house had been blown away in a blizzard. When I woke up from the dream, I would feel terribly blank and alone because no one ever even knew I was gone. I used to cry myself to sleep at night. I don't remember how old I was, or when I quit having the nightmares, or when I quit crying myself to sleep. It was probably the same time I

decided I didn't care what happened in the family anymore, that I wasn't going to be affected or hurt by it ever again."

Margaret had abandonment dreams. Many Children of Alcoholics have nightmares. And even if they haven't experienced such dreams in childhood, many people will have them in their adulthood. Margaret's dreams were most frequently about being alone or being left alone. While abandonment is a major dream theme, powerlessness and scenes of being terrified are also common.

Margaret attended Catholic schools for twelve years. She had a boyfriend.

"Being Catholic, I expected to marry this boyfriend. After all, being sexual and being Catholic meant you would get married."

But then the boyfriend broke up with Margaret. She was devastated. It was at this time she began to drink and use drugs.

JOE

Age: 54
Mother: Co-dependent
Father: Alcoholic
Birth Order: Only child
Raised: South
Socioeconomic Status: Middle class

Joe's story reflects the life of a practicing chemically dependent person who begins his recovery by looking at Adult Child issues first. It was during his ACOA recovery process that Joe recognized that he was also chemically dependent.

Joe was raised with a violent and emotionally abusive alcoholic father and a mother who suffered from severe emotional problems.

JOE:

"I have a key word for my childhood: terror. I grew up terrified — of the violence, the yelling, the screaming, the rage, and the battling that went on in my home. My father was physically abusive to my mother and to me. He would also abuse me through silence. He would withdraw from me — abandon me by refusing to speak to me.

"There was the terror of being isolated, abandoned, of being disliked, of being alone, of not being okay, of not being wanted, of being responsible for my parents' problems. Somehow I learned that if I could be perfect, there would be no problems in my home."

This need to be perfect, and his deep sense of isolation, overflowed into Joe's dealings with other children.

"Even in kindergarten, and all through grade school, I felt this separation; I felt that I'd never belonged, that I was always in the outside looking in. I never felt accepted. I always felt rejected."

The emotional chaos and lack of support and attention that Joe had to face at home left him without any clues about how the rest of the world interacted socially.

"I can remember never knowing how to do things. Never knowing how to act, never knowing where to stand, or what to say, or how to talk, or what to wear. I didn't know how to be popular, how to be sociable, how to get along with other people. I spent most of my childhood in isolation. I read a lot. I read whatever I could. I read alone. I read when I was around others. I was frightened, and reading offered me solace. I would also ride my bicycle. I would ride and ride and ride and ride. I would ride anywhere and nowhere, just to be riding away from it all."

The one social outlet Joe had that was comforting was time spent with his cousins. Joe was an only child, and he had an aunt and uncle with five daughters. He would often ride his bicycle to their home.

"It felt good there. We played. Sometimes it got so busy with all of those kids that I would withdraw, but it was a way to be away from home and not alone. Besides, they did give me attention."

Being an only child made Joe's challenge even greater. Like many only children, he experienced even greater loneliness and isolation. Yet he could break through the isolation, and he found support through a more stable family. But having to return to his own family sabotaged his ability to reach out and find comfort and protection through others.

Joe also found solace playing Little League baseball.

"I played rather well. I was a natural hitter. My mom was supportive in that she arranged for me to have uniforms and the transportation to get to games, but my dad wasn't the least bit interested. When I moved into high school and then changed schools, I didn't play ball anymore. I was afraid of the new kids, it was a larger school, and there was no reinforcement from my parents or anyone to play."

Joe says that at an early age he adopted the attitude *"Nothing ever works out anyway, so why try."* This overwhelming sense of powerlessness is characteristic of many COAs. Joe's attitude pushed him into a pattern of starting projects but never finishing them or following through — such as with baseball, as a student, with careers, and even marriage. This,too, is common for many COAs.

Joe describes himself as playing each of the roles one often finds in an alcoholic family, which is typical of the only child.

"I was the clown. I would cut up in school. I was more disruptive than harmful. I was the irresponsible one. I had learned early on that I would never be good enough, so I was a genuinely lazy kid. I wouldn't feed the dog. I wouldn't rake the leaves. I wouldn't do the schoolwork, at least until I was harassed. At home I always felt as if I were in the way,that things were my fault. I always asked myself — and still do at times today — 'Why didn't my dad like me? What did I do wrong?' At school I was the scapegoat, often the butt of heavy teasing and jokes."

As an adult, when Joe was in college for the second time, he moved into the super-responsible role, into workaholism, and into perfectionism.

"I could play any role. And I played them one right after another, never knowing who I was, and never being me."

By the time Joe was a teenager, the insanity and abuse in his family was completely out of control. In despair Joe fantasized about suicide. This is a common reality for many children in troubled families.

"I didn't really know what was going on except that I knew the whole thing was nuts and I hated it. My high school years were the worst of all. My father's rage increased; my mother's hysteria increased. I hated my father's drinking. I hated my mother's hysteria. I wanted out, and I did a lot of fantasizing about that. If I died, how would they feel? I wanted to die. I wanted to kill myself, but I never got up the courage to do it."

Most children raised in chemically dependent families don't identify the problems within the family as being alcohol-or drug-related. They believe that they are the problem; or they believe that one parent is bad or that money is the issue. The child is usually convinced that the problem is whatever the parents are putting the blame on or whatever excuses they are using to rationalize their circumstances.

Those children who are able to understand that alcohol is a main contributor to the problem, or who see it as the key issue, often promise themselves and other, *"It will never happen to me! I will make sure I don't drink like my dad. I will never treat my kids the way he treats us. I will be home at night. I will play with my kids."* They are so well intentioned. Ask a young child who sees drinking as a problem in his home if he will drink when he becomes an adult, and he will tell you, *"No!"*

Yet most begin to drink in their teenage years. They drink for the same reasons that their parents drink. They drink to be like their friends. They drink because it is supposed to be fun. They drink to escape, to relax, to deaden the pain. But they drink with the firm belief that they will never become like their parent(s). They rationalize that becoming chemically dependent is the result of no willpower and no self-control.

Whether or not they recognize the problems in their life to be alcohol-related — most Children of Alcoholics will drink or use other drugs. Despite their desire not to be like their parents, they often do repeat their family history.

ROLE OF ALCOHOL

Dennis was a very young teenager when he discovered that drinking provided something he felt was missing in his life.

DENNIS:

"When I was thirteen, I took my first drink. It was at a cousin's wedding, and I wanted to be like the grown-ups. I hated the taste, but I kept on drinking. Then I felt the glow, and — it worked! At one point I hit one of my cousins and took a swing at my dad. He decked me, but I still thought I was having a great time.

"Every time I drank after that, I would get sick as a dog. But I would swear on a stack of Bibles that I would still do it again. I got drunk because I had a hole in my gut so big, and when I drank that first time it got filled up. It was the solution. I filled up the hole with booze and then with drugs. It worked. That was all I knew. Nobody paid any attention to my drinking. They thought it was cute, or they didn't notice."

Dennis continued to drink more and more and then moved on to other drugs.

"There was only one reason that I ever ingested alcohol — that was to get blitheringly numb. That's what I wanted to be. My friends and I decided that alcohol was 'uncool'; it was something that our parents used. So we started taking other drugs. I eventually got into doing PCP, which could wipe out any type of feeling. I could decide what to feel. I felt relaxed, not so manic or intense.

"Even heroin addicts were afraid to take PCP in my dosages, and that made me feel powerful. People saw me as crazy, but that was okay. Drugs helped me feel a part of my user friends. People used to laugh and call me 'Loadie' or 'Stoney.' " I wanted to wear that name as a star on my lapel. I looked up to those people. They were fun, cool — especially cool — and I wanted to be like them and liked by them. So I smoked a lot of pot, did acid, speed, PCP and cocaine.

LISA:

Lisa did not drink or use drugs until her marriage ended when she was twenty-nine. She said she may have had one or two drinks in the course of a year, but she was not even a social drinker.

"I was so repulsed by my husband's drinking, and I didn't want to become like my mother. It simply did not occur to me to drink. I didn't want anything to do with alcohol."

When Lisa's marriage ended, she had custody of all four children. She had a full-time job at a telephone company and soon became involved with a married man. She said that his being married was safe for her and prevented her from marrying again. It also kept her from feeling so weak and frightened that she'd be tempted to go back to her husband. She said she thought drinking was what single people did. She felt as if she'd been let out of prison, and it was her turn to live. That's when she began to drink.

"Alcohol helped me to cope. I just seemed to fit in better when I drank, and I could finally talk to people. It was fun and exciting to me in the beginning. It gave me courage. I wasn't afraid or shy anymore. My mom and I could even communicate a little. I thought that drinking was the thing to do. I just wanted to have fun."

Within two years, Lisa felt her life was *"out of control."* One son was getting loaded a lot, another son told her he was having sexual problems, another wanted to move back to his father's. She felt as if she were a failure. All of this was coinciding with her slide into alcoholism.

"I remember drinking at a bar after work one day and someone asking me if I was getting drunk. I said no, that I was just running and trying to cope. I had become the one thing I had never wanted to be — just like my mother! I was unpredictable, belligerent, and obnoxious. I had no fear. I would fight with whatever man or woman got in my way."

Lisa was to drink alcoholically for the next eight years.

BOB:

"By the time I reached the age when I first began experimenting with alcohol, around sixteen or so, I'd seen enough alcohol to float a small country. Everywhere I went, my father drank. He loved to eat out, and he was always drinking in the restaurants. He drank in the bars, and I would have to go pick him up. He was forever late to family gatherings or school events because of his drinking. But my exposure to my father's excessive drinking made drinking seem normal to me."

As it was for Dennis and Lisa, alcohol was an immediate answer for Bob. Alcohol was an answer to the problems and questions that were never safe to pose.

"By the time I was in college, I thought it was okay to have a drink every night before going to bed. I doubt that there was a night in the next fifteen years that I did not drink. It didn't strike me that no one else in the dorm had a drink every day. I didn't think it odd to take a bottle along on a trip just in case I couldn't get access to liquor. I didn't think it was odd to put liquor in a mouthwash bottle so no one would know what it was. I'd had a nodding acquaintance with alcohol at an early age, so it was easier to ignore the early-warning signs of my own alcoholism.

"I believe I drank, in part, to relax, to relieve pain and to hide from alienation and vague feelings of anxiety. But the problem was bigger than that. I drank to get rid of, to hide, or to mask the way I felt. Looking back now, I know I drank to relieve myself of my Adult Child issues. I drank to feel better. I knew I was screwing up, but I didn't know what to do.

"I also used to drink because I felt guilty about drinking. Yet I couldn't stop. I felt so unhappy knowing I shouldn't be drinking, yet I couldn't not drink.

"In college I was a compulsive studier. I clearly had a problem with alcohol, but I managed to function well enough to graduate fifth in my law school class. It was very important for me to succeed and do well. I was always so terrified that I was flunking out. School was

the only way I knew to prove that I was worthwhile. I was trying to prove to others, but even more so to myself, that I was okay. I did have fun at school, but mostly that involved drinking. In the end my drinking and the demands of law school took its toll. I wouldn't ever want to go through that again. I remember flying to see my girlfriend one weekend and hoping the plane would crash so that I could get out of this whole thing honorably."

Bob's drinking gave him something in common with his father and sometimes provided a bond between them that didn't exist in other ways. However, his father's drinking also created a desire in Bob to separate himself from his father's behavior.

"I probably felt closest to Dad when we were both drinking. The alcohol melted away both of our inhibitions, and in a way we could talk more easily then. But I had to catch Dad when he was in the convivial phase of his drinking, and that never lasted long."

Bob married in his last year of law school.

"Anna came from a loving family that drank normally. Things got better for a while. Being with Anna, I wasn't so lonely, I felt better about myself. I adopted her family and spent a lot of time with her father and brother. In essence I tried to substitute Anna's family for my own. I came to regard my family as a biological trap. At this time my work was going well, but soon my drinking became even worse.

"I really didn't have the ability to control it. I never wanted to drink in front of my wife, so I created a lot of projects that took me away from her. I used to go to the cellar a lot to work on things. It got so bad that I even started to urinate in jars downstairs so I wouldn't have to go upstairs for her to see me. I was also experiencing blackouts."

MARGARET:

"The first time I remember drinking was after school at a girlfriend's house. I wasn't drinking for any particular reason. It was what teenagers did. I wasn't a very happy child. I was pretty aimless. So, anyway, here I was. We were drinking screwdrivers; I don't remember how many, but I do remember walking home and noticing

that my lip was numb. I thought it felt wonderful, and I wished that I could always feel that way."

In addition to drinking, Margaret began to smoke marijuana.

"The first time I smoked pot, I thought, This is great stuff for me! My mind seemed to open up to new ideas, and I saw the world in a whole different light. It wasn't long before I was using pot almost every day, and then daily just to maintain. When I drank, it was for total oblivion. I also used relationships so I wouldn't have to feel lonely. I was very promiscuous."

After high school, Margaret took four years to complete two years of college. She was basically consumed with alcohol and drugs.

"I went to class and partied a lot. I took mescaline,blotter acid, psychedelics, speed, cocaine, alcohol, marijuana. For a while I did some small-time selling of marijuana. I took whatever a boyfriend or dealer friend would give me."

When she was twenty-five Margaret joined the Air Force, looking for some *"orderly direction"* in her life. She had always thought she would have her life together by the time she was twenty-one, but it took until she was twenty-five to wake up and realize she was not getting there. Yet she continued to drink and smoke pot on a daily basis. Her promiscuity interfered with her ability to get certain clearances. She dealt with that by marrying shortly out of basic training.

"I married a heavy drinker and knew it, but I thought we would quit together. Not long after we were married, I went for help on the pretense of my husband's needing the help."

JOE:

By his later high school years, Joe was emotionally desperate. His use of alcohol was an immediate love affair.

"During my senior year in high school I was invited to a fraternity rush party at a local college. It was there that I took my first real drink. It was beer,and I loved it. I was an alcoholic from the first swallow, a

practicing alcoholic. I had been a time bomb waiting to explode. I got very drunk and blacked out. I carried on like a real idiot, from what people told me. I woke up the next morning with a bad hangover and no recollection of what had happened. What amazed me, though, was that I was sort of a hero with this group of fraternity people. I had immediately found a friend in alcohol. I had found a way to get through one more day without killing myself. I had found a way to be accepted. I had found a way to be a part of a group, to be popular. I had found something to fix me, something to fill up that horrible empty hole inside, something to make me feel adequate, okay, and able to cope."

Joe spent his college years binge drinking every weekend.

"I never drank except with total insanity. I never drank for any purpose except to wreck my brain. I could never control my drinking."

Finally Joe's grades suffered from his drinking, During his junior year he dropped out to work in the oil fields. He finally went back to college to study engineering.

"I got serious about my studies and discovered my second real fix: accomplishment, achievement, good grades. I was either obsessed with working or binge drinking. Because I would do it only twice a month or so, I still had the illusion that I was controlling my drinking, despite my bizarre, stupid, and life-threatening behavior when I was drunk."

Joe got married and continued to go to school to obtain his doctorate in order to teach at the university level.

"I was very much a workaholic. I had also become sexually obsessed, and I was a compulsive spender. I would always grab anything to fix me — by bachelor's degree, my master's, a Ph.D., a wife, a child, another child, a drink, a new car, something to buy, something to spend. I also became addicted to self-defeat, addicted to self-destructive behavior.

"I got a job teaching at a university. This whole time period was one of outrageous drinking and very egotistical, aggressive, and antisocial behavior. My lack of responsibility, my compulsive spend-

ing, and my drinking began to dominate my life. I became more and more confused and more and more terrified. My wife and I divorced after sixteen years of a marriage that had always been rocky. There was unhappiness from the start. She fit my pattern that 'No matter what I did it was never good enough.' and I was obsessive, compulsive, and addicted."

Joe said he didn't participate much at all in the raising of his children, who were eleven and thirteen when he left the family.

"I hardly realized I had children. I was totally preoccupied with myself. Although I did want to provide for my family, my life-style interfered with that.

"As each one of my fixes failed, I would look for another one. I became addicted to self-help books. I kept thinking that I would find the magic secret that would fix me, the thing that was going to make me okay. When I finally ran out of fixes, I hit bottom. No one would have guessed except a few of those closest to me that, despite my outward appearance, on the inside I was terrified, panic-stricken, and functioning at the edge of survival. I was lacking any sense of self-worth or self-esteem. Everything was disintegrating, everything."

The Bottom

Chemical dependency is said to be a cunning, baffling disease, and I believe this is true. One of the most confusing aspects of chemical dependency is how it varies in visibility.

Joe's addictions, although not so blatant to him, were obvious to those around him. Dennis was so lost in his chemicals, he had to have someone else — his father — intervene. Bob was disintegrating quietly, his disease apparent only to his wife.

It's unlikely that Margaret would have found anyone to help address her issue because she surrounded herself with others similar to her. Yet instinctively, when she hit her own bottom, she knew there was help out there — even though she moved toward recovery by seeking it for her husband. Lisa's drinking was obvious to her and those around her, but it would take getting *"tired of being sick and tired"* before she sought help.

ADULTHOOD AND RECOVERY

Recovery is the process that begins when the chemically dependent people begin to realize that alcohol and/or drugs is the source of the problems in their lives. Along with this realization comes the insight that stopping alcohol or drug usage is not as simple as deciding to control it or willing it away — they are going to need help in order to stop. The hardest part is understanding that recovery means total abstinence from all mind-changing chemicals.

Some people seek help very willingly after a period of physical, mental, emotional, spiritual and social devastation. Others seek help grudgingly, wanting it but preferring to control how they get and use the assistance offered. Still others seek help only to satisfy another person's desires.

When one is chemically dependent, that's the issue that's nearly always going to have to be addressed first. Yet the problem is more complex for people like Joe. He was a compulsive spender, sexually obsessive, and a workaholic in addition to being addicted to alcohol and other drugs. His family life had been severely affected by all of these issues. Where does such a person begin recovery? Unfortunately many people begin with the money, sex, work, or family issues without identifying and focusing on the chemical addiction. Very often they spend years not finding answers. This is made more difficult by the fact that there is a tendency for addicted people and those around them to want to focus on anything but the addictions. Because it is such a primary addiction, alcoholism and/or drug abuse is the one issue dependent people will fight the hardest to maintain. The result is that they are never able to recover in the one area that offers them the greatest opportunity to recover in all the other areas of their lives.

We revisit Dennis, Lisa, Bob, Margaret, and Joe as they describe their recovery process. They tell us what led them to recovery from their chemical dependency and how their Adult Child issues interfaces with recovery from this dependency.

DENNIS

Age: 32
Partner Status: Single
Occupation: Actor
Recovery Process: AA; twelve year sober ACOA, therapy

Dennis got sober when he was twenty years old. Dennis's father had become sober the year before, and he was instrumental in bringing Dennis to Alcoholics Anonymous.

DENNIS:

"I hated my dad when he first got sober. I resented him and resisted him. But my life was truly unmanageable. I hurt, and I didn't know how to take the pain away. Not even the drugs were doing it anymore. Finally my Dad intervened. All I'd ever wanted was for my dad to be there, and there he was. I didn't understand what he was saying, but I had no energy left to fight him. I was really screwed up."

Dennis' father played a strong father role for a person so newly sober. He saw his son's addiction and reached out to help. Those not familiar with alcoholism recovery might assume this is an obvious response. But Dennis' father had been alcoholic a long time. Many people who have only been sober a year are not yet able to influence their families. In fact, often out of guilt, they take a very passive role. Dennis was fortunate because his father was not willing to be passive.

"I went to my first AA meeting and did what they said. I didn't use, and I didn't drink. I don't remember much about those first few months, but I know I liked feeling part of a family."

Alcoholics Anonymous gave Dennis the sense of belonging he had yearned for as a child. It became a family unit for him. While that may sound understandable because he was only twenty, it is often just as true for the person who is older.

"AA parented me as my parents had not been able to. The slogans and the Twelve Steps offered me a path that made a lot of sense to me. I had been raised Catholic and I liked the spiritual part of the program. I was ready. So I spent the next ten years growing up.

"When I was thirty years old — and ten years sober — I found things still weren't as they seemed they should be. I was still frightened a lot. I felt lonely. I could never really put together an intimate relationship. I had this sense that I was doing what I was supposed to do, but that I wasn't able to decide what I wanted in life. I had heard about Adult Child self-help groups and decided to try one."

Dennis' Alcoholic/Addict and Adult Child Issues:

Dennis had some very specific work he needed to do in ACOA about his anger at his dad. First of all, that anger was getting in the way of how he was relating to his father. Second, in some ways AA was becoming the symbol of how he felt about his father. Dennis needed to address the anger at his father in order not to push AA out of his life.

DENNIS:

"I loved my father so much when I was a kid, but socially and emotionally he abandoned me. I was never able to address that issue. One day, after I started going to ACOA meetings, I broke down and started accusing my father and calling him names. I did it again six months later. When I let him have it a third time, expressing the hurt I felt and crying and crying, my dad finally said my anger was okay, but in time I would need to realize that he had done the best he could.

"That's when I came to the realization that these issues were my issues. I went to him and apologized for my behavior. He cried in my arms. It was so powerful. I felt such incredible love. It was a real catharsis to be able to confront him with my feelings, and I don't put the blame on him anymore."

For Dennis it was important to confront his father. He was also fortunate that his father was able to hear what he had to say. Someday Dennis may also want to say some things to his mother or work on issues related to his mother.

"My mother is also in recovery — she got sober the same day I did. But I always related more to her co-dependency issues than to her alcoholism."

Like most Adult Children, Dennis had focused his internal work on the parent whose loss of relationship was more blatant. There is nothing wrong or hurtful in that, it's natural. Yet in time Adult Children are able to see that it is a family disease, and there are issues to be resolved around the nonalcoholic codependent parent, and in Dennis' case the less visible chemically and codependent dependent parent, too.

Dennis not only found friends in AA, he clearly responded to the basics of the program: the Twelve Steps.

"The Twelve Steps are the meat and potatoes of both the AA and ACOA programs. But after ten years of being sober I found an identification in Adult Child self-help groups that has been vital to my recovery.

"In ACOA I have found a place to talk about my fears, sadnesses, and anger. Prior to ACOA I had not learned to deal with my feelings. I was still denying my feelings even after ten years of sobriety. Feelings left over from childhood were running rampant and intruding on my adult life. Denying my feelings was as self-destructive to my recovery as the denial of my alcoholism had been to my sobriety. I had become emotionally paralyzed."

Dennis had found that until he addressed the feelings he had repressed in his childhood, it would continue to be difficult for him to identify and express his present-day feelings. As a youngster he only knew how to medicate his feelings. Yet, at thirty, he still had not yet learned how to be safe with his feelings.

"In the program, dealing with the issue of God was helpful for me. God has the power to take away obsession. But I still needed to make that connection with all my obsessions — lust, caffeine, people, chaos, overactivity, negative and abusive people. I knew I needed to 'let go, and let God,' but I needed something more. In ACOA I was able to find that missing link.

"In ACOA, it felt safe to talk about your past. I heard others talk about their childhood, and I identified with what they were saying. I'd not had the experience of talking honestly about my growing-up years before. Talking about the past takes the power out of childhood messages.

"I had internalized messages such as 'My needs are not important.' 'Boys don't cry,' and 'I have to do everything by myself.' In ACOA I learned where these beliefs had come from and had the opportunity to counter them. But first I had to recognize what they were. Identifying with other people has a tremendous value.

"By learning to understand my feelings, I've made tremendous gains in my ability to maintain relationships. When I came into ACOA I was clearly in a relationship crisis. I am now learning to share how I feel with other people. While I am in a relationship, I still find intimacy intimidating — but I'm working at being more responsive to my girlfriend's needs and not being so selfish and showing my emotions more. Today I am ready to make a commitment to the woman I have been in love with for the past four years.

"I'm also working at learning how to play. Up to now I've always needed to be accomplishing something — or acting as if I was. By knowing my feelings better, I'm more aware of my needs. I can relax more. I'm also able to be available to others because I don't spend so much energy protecting myself. That has helped me in my relationship with my dad.

"Through ACOA, I've been able to work out a lot of the stuff with my father. Today he's a doting grandfather. And he gives to both his kids and his grandchildren — he wants to make up for the time that

we lost. We do things together. I can spend the whole day with him. I never could do that before."

Both the AA and ACOA programs are important to Dennis' recovery, and he recognizes that each program has something special to offer.

"I'm going to AA and using my sponsor. I go because my foundation is there, the basics are there. It's a stronger program in the Steps. I also attend one or two ACOA meetings a week and see a therapist with my partner so we can work on some of our relationship issues, such as communication.

"The first two and a half years in ACOA I developed a better sense of my feelings. I can cry when I need to. But I still need to find a balance — sometimes I focus too much on feelings.

"I do relate to my AA program, and I believe that ACOA has enhanced my AA program. I've done a better inventory. I've worked the Steps harder. I learned a better God consciousness. I began to feel God, not just know about God. Since this time I have also found my faith in God through church to be a major support to me. I had been so angry as a child with God and have struggled, but today I have given my Higher Power my trust.

"I'm a stronger person. I can face life better. I can go the extra mile. I have a better capacity for closure.

"Recovery is a process. Much of this recovery has been difficult, but it is happening. It's a better way of life. I feel the comfort that comes from it. Today I can sit and be quiet. I'm less depressed, less angry — far less angry — and that makes me more loving."

LISA

Age: 42
Partner Status: Single, three living adult children
Occupation: Student
Recovery Process: AA; six years sober, ACOA, therapy

After eight years of drinking, Lisa hit her bottom. She called her brother-in-law, who was in AA, and went with him to her first meeting. What she remembers about that meeting was the laughter. She said she identified with the feelings and knew she could be helped. When she was close to a year sober, she relapsed and drank for another nine months. She says she wasn't convinced that she was alcoholic. However, after several months of drinking, lengthy blackouts began to convince her. She went back to the AA program.

LISA:

"In the first year of my sobriety, I never understood how being the Child of an Alcoholic had anything to do with my alcoholism. I was just trying to get sober and have some kind of consistency and order in my life. I just concentrated on the Twelve Steps and going to meetings. Finally I was able to laugh and to think clearly. But at the same time I was beginning to feel depressed, alone, and afraid again. I knew I had to keep trying in order to get my life together. Yet my whole life I had tried to be strong and never ask for help."

It was best that Lisa's initial focus was on getting sober, for she would soon have to face two major traumas. In doing so, she found that she now had the skills to cope without drinking — in the past that would have been her first and only option.

The first trauma occurred when Lisa's sixteen year old son fatally overdosed. She was one year and twenty-nine days sober. This is when

Lisa realized that she had more to deal with than the issue of her own sobriety.

"My world fell apart. I didn't drink over it, but I thought I was going to lose my mind."

In addition to dealing with the tragic loss of her son, Lisa became aware of another trauma in her life that she had suppressed until then. She had been an incest victim as a child.

After a relatively short time sober, Lisa began to have flashbacks of being sexually abused by her father. Then, after her father died, she was molested twice more by different men in her neighborhood. Awareness of this abuse is still something new for Lisa; the memories are continuing to present themselves.

Alcohol was no longer an option for Lisa in dealing with the death of her son. She needed to openly grieve his tragic loss. But out of this depth of honesty she found the courage to face the sexual abuse — a secret that had remained hidden for years.

Lisa also had the strength to seek help in dealing with the loss of her son and the incest. She had learned in her first year of sobriety that it was okay to ask for help.

Lisa's Alcoholic and Adult Child Issues:

"I had not been aware of ACOA until very recently, and my sobriety and my recovery program have changed dramatically since the time of my son's death. I have learned that getting sober is not enough to have a meaningful life. I have had to deal with each and every issue of my childhood and rebuild a foundation for myself other than the one I was taught. The past four years of therapy, along with the ACOA program, have saved my life.

"In dealing with the incest issue, I have also begun to deal with my Adult Child issues, which I feel are directly related to my alcoholism. Everything I was taught when I was little I have repeated as an Adult Child. My drinking was no different. I drank to cope, to be a part of my family, but my feelings were ignored. I was never heard and always felt afraid. When I drank I could talk, feel, and be heard.

I would never have been able to communicate with people or deal with the stress otherwise. My mother drank to cope and to communicate. I did the same thing. I never realized how much I had become like her until I got sober.

"Through recovery, I can now say how I feel most of the time without being angry or afraid. I can feel what my feelings are instead of being numb. I know that my feelings are valid. I am able to make decisions for myself and feel good about those decisions most of the time. I no longer need someone else to tell me how I'm feeling.

"I am able to look inside of me and not be ashamed of who I am. I no longer feel the need to run away and hide from who I am. I am happy to say that I love me today for who I am and not for what I thought I was supposed to be. I have my own identity, and I am forever grateful for this. I can trust my own judgment and even trust a couple of other people in my life today.

"When I was little I was never able to think like a child. I always thought like an adult. The messages I received about love and friendship were that they were mixed with pain and masochism, confusion and betrayal. I had to relearn about love. I have had to redefine morals. I have had to redefine spiritual beliefs. I am learning about boundaries. I am learning about choices. I have learned I am not crazy. I know it is okay to feel, to cry, to be angry. I have learned I don't need to be abused to be loved. I have also learned that life can be fun."

Lisa has learned a lot in the past six years. At times people question how such a transformation is possible. The answer is that Lisa had direction and support — and she was willing to risk and willing to follow direction. She used several different tools, but they were compatible — therapy, Alcoholics Anonymous, and ACOA. Her therapist was also knowledgeable and respectful of the alcoholism recovery process.

By facing her own alcoholism and recognizing the Adult Child issues in her life, Lisa has been able to begin dealing with alcoholism as a family disease.

"My life is my own, and I am responsible for it. I can see the damage I have done with my own children. My two sons are both chemically dependent. My oldest, I feel, has a drinking problem. He doesn't think so. My youngest is addicted to marijuana and alcohol. My daughter just recently admitted that she is an alcoholic, although she is not ready to give up the bottle just yet.

"My mother has not been through a recovery process but today due to age and health problems is abstinent. While my mother has not changed significantly, because of my own recovery, I have come to forgive and to love her.

"By dealing with my own alcoholism and my ACOA issues, I have been able to share my experiences and discoveries with the other members of my family. My twin, Laney, and her daughters have begun to read some Adult Child literature. They are not willing to admit that there is a problem. Today it is my life's aim, and their hope, that the generations to come won't subscribe to not feeling, not talking, and not trusting.

"Knowing that I must be honest, and having a trust in God, has been my salvation. The Twelve Step program has allowed me to have a recovery."

It is a difficult challenge to get sober, to begin to address your own Adult Child/incest issues, to respond to the major trauma of losing a child, and then be open to looking at the next generation in your family. To keep these potentially overwhelming issues in perspective, one needs a solid foundation of recovery and the willingness to stay close to the program.

BOB

Age: 37
Partner Status: Married, two children
Occupation: Attorney
Recovery Process: Outpatient Alcoholism treatment; AA; three and a half years sober, Adult Child group therapy

Bob sought out Alcoholics Anonymous and periodically made attempts to be sober. Like many alcoholics, he attempted sobriety for several years before he was able to maintain it.

BOB:

"Prior to my being married, I had once walked myself into a central office of Alcoholics Anonymous and told this man there that there was something wrong with my drinking, that I didn't have the ability to stop. He offered to take me to a meeting. I went, and for a whole summer I didn't drink. But I quit going to meetings because I felt I was different from the other people there. In my own mind I wasn't ready to stop. I then continued to drink for another couple of years."

Bob drank during social occasions, but his refuge was the cellar of his house. That was his private bar.

"A few times my wife had approached me while I was in the cellar. Pretty much aware of what I was doing, she told me she was concerned for me. She said that what I was doing was not normal and not healthy. One day she mentioned that she wanted me to go to the church to listen to a talk about alcohol problems. That led to an assessment by an alcoholism counselor. Then I went back to AA, but I didn't like it."

Bob himself had been periodically questioning his drinking. Otherwise he would not have so readily responded to his wife's confrontation. Yet being chemically dependent and a driven Adult Child, he once again would struggle against the help that was available.

"I developed a home group, but I wasn't ready or able to use it. I would not drink as long as it was a typical day, but I drank on the holidays and whenever I went to my parents. I found plenty of reasons to make exceptions for being able to drink.

"I struggled with recovery for my alcoholism for some time. I knew something was wrong, but I didn't really know what to do about it. Although I was going to AA, in reality I was holding on by my fingertips. I started having a relapse every two months or so — not serious blowout drunks, but just drinking even though I knew it was part of my program not to drink.

"A friend of mine in AA had just completed an Adult Child course and thought I might be interested, so I signed up. I was searching for something, although at the time I didn't realize that what I was searching for was my own acceptance and surrender. Together with the other people in the Adult Child group, we agreed not to use mood-altering chemicals. No problem for me — I thought — I was in AA and a recovering alcoholic. It didn't take much, just a little truth, and I cried and cried. I was a little boy full of tears. I was getting a lot out of the program, but I wasn't sober. Finally my therapist convinced me to enroll in an outpatient program for my own alcoholism. This led me to the formal treatment that has made the difference for me."

It is difficult to ascertain whether or not Bob was an alcoholic who simply had not surrendered, or if his Adult Child issues of feeling different, and anger at his father, were interfering with his ability to get sober. But it is more obvious that the initial grief he experienced in speaking about his Adult Child issues were connected with the surrender that facilitated his sobriety.

In alcoholism treatment he was advised not to focus on his dad's alcoholism, but rather on his own. At that time Bob's focus on his father was becoming a diversion from focusing on himself. The lessening of his grief was important Adult Child work, and it enhanced the beginning of his recovery. But now his continued focus on his father only served to keep his focus off taking responsibility for himself.

"I struggled for a good while with wanting to focus on my father. But I finally gave in because I was tired of fighting. I was simply exhausted. It was safer for me to deal with his alcoholism — less shameful, perhaps — than facing my own. The Adult Child issues were the magnet to treatment. But once there, they were an obstacle that had to be moved aside, to be returned to at a later date."

Bob's Alcoholic and Adult Child Issues:

By recognizing the problems that he faced as an Adult Child, Bob found that he had to deal with the issues of control, trust, and risk taking as a part of his recovery.

"I'd always had a 'Don't take any risks — don't rock the boat' philosophy. Expect the worst, I thought, and be happy if something better happens. It was a pretty gloomy outlook on life, but I thought it reduced my chances of getting hurt. In recovery, I've had to learn to reach out to people, to take a few chances. I've had to risk disclosure so that I can clean house emotionally and let others come to know and love me. I feel that intimacy is worth having, but it requires taking risks.

"I have trouble trusting people. At the office I check the math of junior lawyers and recheck documents for the hearings that I do. At home I check to see if the doors are locked before I go to sleep, even if someone else tells me they've locked them. I find I'm getting better about these things. The whole treatment process for me involved letting someone else decide what might be better for me, learning to do what I was told, and trying to see if someone else's approach would work better."

Letting other people be a part of one's recovery process creates a lot of vulnerability. Disclosing to others, depending on others, is very frightening when one has never felt safe doing that. So often we don't even know how closed we are until we are given an opportunity to look at ourselves symbolically through a medium such as art therapy.

"I struggled to do this recovery business myself for several years before I underwent formal treatment. Even in recovery, when I drew pictures in art therapy, I drew only myself. I drew in no counselors, no helpers, no support group, even though I was in their midst and they had their arms outstretched to help me over the bumps."

Bob has had to work on his ACOA tendency to see things in extremes, with no middle ground.

"I often see things as black or white, all right or all wrong. I want to categorize a thing or a situation and then put it where it belongs, in this slot or that one. I tend to do this rather quickly, often without giving the issue I'm classifying the time and attention it deserves. It's been hard learning that while some things are black and white, other things are gray.

"Long ago, because of my father's alcoholism, I categorized alcoholism as bad. In my childhood, certainly no good ever came from it for me, only problems. Now I understand that it is a disease, and good things can come from recovering from it.

"I've also had to realize that my recovery may be different from another person's. There are many roads that lead to recovery. It's not a cake recipe where there is precisely one cup of this and one cup of that. It's more like a stew where you start with what you have in the refrigerator. I've learned that my way isn't for everyone. Now I can share my thoughts about what has worked for me, but I'm not insulted if someone doesn't do it my way. Life and recovery are more multi-faceted than that. I won't die if things aren't a certain way. I'm learning to loosen up, to let go of some of the rigidity and stiffness I learned as a child and still carry with me today. Those were, and still are, things that impede my recovery."

Bob is now able to identify and be a little humorous about how his perfectionism can interfere in the quality of his sobriety. Perfectionism is often a way for people to compensate for feeling defective, for feeling shame.

"I keep struggling with my tendency to work for a 'perfect recovery.' I get compulsive about it. I have a three-by-card file box with the Twelve Steps on index cards, though to my credit I don't have much on the index cards. I have Twelve Step tapes that I listen to in my car on my way to business meetings.

"There's a risk that my perfectionism will spoil the pudding. I remember reading the inspirational goals of Twenty-Four Hours a Day (meditation book familiar to recovering alcoholics) and being frustrated that I had not achieved them yet. Finally I switched to a different book, but not until I threw the book against the bathroom wall."

The insights Bob has gained through work on his Adult Child issues have had a strong impact on his recovery as an alcoholic. He has specifically looked at his need to look good, his control issues, his guilt and shame, and now his feelings about his father.

"My need for acceptance and reassurance and my general desire to 'look good' had make it difficult for me to be honest in recovery. I'm getting over it, but it's still hard for me to say something if it might hurt someone, even if it needs to be said.

"I sometimes attempt to control people by trying to get them to do what I think they should. Although I'm getting better about it. Now I recognize when I do it. On the last two occasions in after care (post treatment therapy), people have rejected my efforts. But we talked about it. And once I got over feeling rejected, I felt relieved and happy that I didn't have to be responsible for them.

"I'm a little too comfortable with guilt. I feel guilty about things I'm not responsible for. So now I'm making an effort not to be responsible for other people's recoveries and other problems over which I have no control.

"I was mortified when my wife told her parents about my problems and my alcoholism treatment. I felt they would see me as less than

perfect. I was still trying to look good. They responded very appropriately and positively, though. I realize that I cannot talk myself out of their love for me."

It is very powerful for alcoholics feeling shame to discover that others truly care and love them. But in order for Bob to learn that, he first had to be honest with himself and others. While he was initially horrified that his wife was breaking family denial when she told her parents, this revelation led Bob to being able to accept their love.

"Embracing the disease concept of alcoholism has helped me go a long way toward forgiving my father.

"Today I understand that my father is also an Adult Child who has the disease of alcoholism. Yet, it still hurts me to watch all of that when I'm powerless to change it. I feel as if my father is a million miles away. He's like one of those stars whose light comes to Earth from millions of miles away. When it comes, it is faint. It has to be a clear night, and you have to wait an eternity for it to come. I try to break in there with hugs, tell him I love him. It feels good to me to try, and I do, but I feel frustrated by his lack of response. He doesn't want to be in the same room with me alone. Obviously my recovery threatens him, as does my mother's recovery in Al-Anon."

When an Adult Child is in recovery and the other family members are not, there will be distance in their relationships. It will be frustrating as well. Although Bob can have a relationship with his father, he will need to have fewer expectations, as his father is still alcohol-affected. If he can do this, it will result in less frustration. He's much more likely to have a closer relationship with his mother, as they have in common their mutual involvement in Twelve-Step programs.

"Today, sober for a few years, the only thing I miss about my drinking days is that when I drank with my father we had a bond."

Acknowledging that there was such a significant payoff in his drinking — it offered the only connection with his father — takes a lot of honesty. It's painful to admit that alcohol is the basis of an intimate relationship. Bob will need to own the sadness, and very likely the anger, that will come as a result of this awareness.

"I'm also angry and feel cheated that the disease has taken my father from me. But that's okay. It's okay to feel angry and hurt. I can't rewrite my childhood."

Bob is like the majority of addicted Adult Children, he is the product of second-, third-, and even fourth-generation alcohol/drug-affected thinking and parenting. He cannot rewrite his childhood, but his recovery has begun, and he can rewrite the script for his children.

"I can, however, make things a whole lot different for my children. And today many of my greatest joys are my playing — literally playing — with my children and their friends, and participating in their lives. We have wonderful family meals. Every Sunday we have people over, I cook, we share the food, the kids play. It's a harmony I really like.

"I think the shame I feel over my own alcoholism is a refinement and purification of the shame I felt as a child over my father's alcoholism. On an emotional level, I drank a liquor twice-brewed. To think that I would end up like my father, that my disease could do to my children what his disease did to me, was a prospect too horrible to comprehend. This was the raw meal of shame that I milled and baked into a fine pastry. You'd think this prospect would strengthen my denial. But I feel that the fear of ending up like Dad made it easier for me to admit that I was powerless and ready for a change. I saw the road I was walking down, and I was scared to death.

"It was difficult, though, recognizing what my father and I had in common. I tried hard not to do the things my father did, at least superficially. He drank in bars; I drank only at home. We were always waiting for him to come home; I always came home before I drank. He would cry for help; I would ask for none. Superficially we were different; but underneath we had the same disease.

"My recovery has taught me that I am not my father. I am different. I am thirty-seven; he is sixty-two. I am recovering; he is not. He brought his family full term into their Adult Child issues; I am doing

what I can to break the cycle for my family in my lifetime. Still, deep down, I think my shame for my own alcoholism is stronger because it is an extension of my shame for him."

In recognizing the depth of shame, alcoholics and addicts such as Bob need to remember how important it is to work on recovery in both areas.

"I believe I have to work on my Adult Child issues for my recovery to progress. It's like I'm moving a heavy log. The whole thing is just too heavy to move all at once. To make progress, I have to lift one end up and move it forward, then pick up the other end and move it forward, and then just keep repeating the process.

"Today I recognize that feeling of joy, and I live it. It comes from loving people, and I have a hunch it comes from loving myself and seeing good in myself. It comes from realizing that it is okay to be an alcoholic, and it is wonderful to be a recovering alcoholic."

MARGARET

Age: 35
Partner Status: Married, two children
Occupation: Office manager
Recovery Process: Outpatient & inpatient alcoholism treatment; AA; six years sober, Al-Anon

Within a year of joining the service, Margaret went for help for her husband and his drinking problem. At this time she was also pregnant. Within a few more months she and her husband asked to leave the military, using medical leave as the reason. Margaret's husband simply wanted out, and she didn't know what else to do but follow, even though she says she loved the military. She liked the structure it gave her.

The treatment program asked her, as the spouse, to monitor her own drinking and limit it to no more than three drinks.

MARGARET:

"Now I was pregnant, and yet I clearly didn't want to respond to the three-drink limit. The counselor suggested I go to AA. I instantly thought, I can't go there, that's my Dad's program! I knew AA worked. I had watched it work for thirty-plus years. I wasn't ready."

Margaret gave birth to a baby girl and continued to drink and use. It became clear that she couldn't control her alcohol use. Margaret was exhausted with the emotional, mental, social, and physical struggle characteristic of what so many alcoholics experience prior to surrender. There was no spiritual struggle; she was spiritually bankrupt by then.

At the age of twenty-nine, Margaret decided to quit drinking. A week later she also stopped her drug use. She began going to AA. It was also shortly after that, that she and her husband divorced.

"At first all I know was that I was an alcoholic and that my father was an alcoholic. He had been sober in AA for thirty-eight years when he died, which was two months before I got sober. So, obviously, I was the child of an alcoholic. I did fine in AA for two years. I didn't have a compulsion, and the people all seemed to understand how I felt and what I was going through. I had found unconditional love and acceptance. But then I began wondering, 'Is this all there is?'"

Margaret knew factually that she was an ACOA. While many people know that to be a fact about themselves, that does not mean they understand how they have been impacted by that family system.

Margaret then married a man she had met in AA, and they moved to a new town. Although she was looking forward to starting a new life, she found it difficult to connect with the people in her new AA meetings. At first she thought that it was just a result of the move and of being in a strange town. But then she began to realize that the problem ran deeper than that.

"I had difficulty sharing my gut feelings in meetings because I really didn't know what my gut feelings were. My sponsor didn't give up, though. She just kept at me, and little by little things began to come out — no real biggies, just little things that I didn't want to look at.

"We would talk about my 'sticking my head in the sand.' I remember as a young girl learning about how the ostrich would stick its head in the sand so the enemy would think that it was a bush. The ostrich wouldn't pull its head out until the enemy had gone away. I really thought that, like the ostrich, if I didn't see it, it wasn't there and couldn't hurt me."

Margaret continued to avoid dealing with her problems until certain events made her confront her feelings.

"My husband, Larry, was going through a custody battle with his ex-wife for their son. I had my daughter from my earlier marriage, and finally his son also moved in with us. We decided that we needed more money, so I went to work full-time. I was offered a job in an alcoholism treatment center as the aftercare treatment secretary. Part of my job was to cover staffing, and I began hearing the staff talk about patients who hadn't dealt with certain issues. I realized that I hadn't dealt with these issues, either, in three years of sobriety."

At this time Margaret's daughter came down with a serious illness, which reinforced the point that counseling was something the whole family needed. Margaret continued to go to AA meetings, but she felt she wasn't getting what she needed out of them. She was finding it more and more difficult to cope with her feelings. She began thinking that Valium would make her feel better, but she knew that that was just another side of her addiction. Finally she sought help through her supervisor at work, who helped her check into a recovery center.

"My first night there, one of the leaders of the group asked me if I'd ever thought of myself as a Child of an Alcoholic. All I could do was cry. That's when I began to work on my co-dependency issues. I began attending Al-Anon meetings in addition to my AA meetings.

Margaret's Alcoholic and Adult Child Issues:

"I truly believe it is almost impossible to be happy, joyous, and free in sobriety if you don't work on your Adult Child issues. And even if you don't know that you have any, they still have a way of surfacing on their own. In AA I sometimes feel alone and different. I'm glad I've found Al-Anon. There are a lot of Adult Children there. I don't know if I could stay sober without both groups.

"I didn't start focusing on my ACOA issues until I was faced with drinking again. There was a co-dependency group available in that program. I never really knew that my co-dependency issues were getting in the way of my recovery until I was hospitalized. And then I did so only because at that point I had to face the fact that just not drinking or using was no longer enough."

Margaret realized that the behavior she had learned as a child in an alcoholic family was making her own recovery more difficult.

"Several things were getting in the way of my recovery. One was my ability to 'look good' and 'act good' even though I was in turmoil. I would do this at work and at AA meetings. Even if I'm pouring my heart out to somebody, I still have a way of coming across as though I'm able to handle it all by myself.

"I've always had difficulty asking for help — on top of an ability to endure intolerable situations for a long time. I stick my head in the sand and keep thinking things will get better or that the problem will go away. I also have trouble identifying my own feelings and my own needs. I'd rather try to 'fix' other people so I don't have to look at myself and take responsibility for what's happening.

"I began reading Adult Child literature and was able to recognize that I had difficulty asking for help; I had difficulty identifying feelings; I preferred to fix others while negating myself; and my enduring intolerable situations had been learned in childhood.

"By recognizing these issues, I've been able to work on them, but it's still very difficult for me. If someone identifies my feelings for me, I can tell if that person's perception is right or not, but I still find it

hard to express those feelings myself. I used to think that the only feelings a person had were happy, sad, glad, and afraid. When I saw a feelings list, I was amazed at how many different feelings there were. I had decided at a very young age that I wasn't ever going to let anyone hurt me again. The only way to do that was not to feel. It has been very hard to unlearn that behavior.

"I've also had a hard time with my need to fix other people. I didn't know you couldn't do that. I thought that if I concentrated on everyone else, I wouldn't have to look at myself. So I concentrated on what was wrong with my husband, my stepson, my work, and the world in general. Thank God for Al-Anon! I still try focusing on other people sometimes, but my Al-Anon meetings bring me right back where I need to be."

Another issue that Margaret had to come to terms with was her denial of her mother's alcoholism and the effects that had on her.

"One of the things I've had to face is the fact that my mother is also an alcoholic. I had always known that my father was, but I had never thought my mother had a drinking problem until I got sober. Even then I never thought her drinking affected me.

"Through my Al-Anon program, I began to explore the feelings I had about my mother's drinking. I realized that even now when she drinks, I get scared and confused. I feel lonely, just the way I did when I was a child. She was never there for me. She was never available to comfort me when I cried. She was never there to help me with my homework. I worry about her health, but I know that I cannot control her drinking. I love her, but when she drinks, the alcohol comes through and I lose her."

Margaret is learning to express her own needs. As an Adult Child, this is something that has always been extremely difficult for her.

"Because as a child I often didn't know what my needs were, they didn't get met. Then I would become angry with other people for not making me feel better. Yet I couldn't tell them what my needs were. I'm now having to deal with the fear of saying those needs out loud.

When I do take the risk, though, people often respond positively. Now I'm able to recognize when I'm sitting on my feelings."

AA and Al-Anon are both essential parts of Margaret's recovery.

"I don't feel I could stay sober by just going to AA meetings. I need help with my ACOA issues, or I'll deceive myself into thinking that if I just took this or that, I wouldn't have to feel that way anymore. My recovery has been a rocky path. I'm grateful for AA, Al-Anon, and the ACOA concepts. While my path is still bumpy, the healing has begun."

JOE

Age: 54
Partner Status: Single, two children
Occupation: Accident investigator
Recovery Process: AA; three years sober, ACOA, Course in Miracles

Joe began drinking in his college years. He was chronically addicted to alcohol, cocaine, and a multitude of other drugs. Not only was he chemically dependent, but his compulsive personality fed into workaholism, sex addiction, and overeating. In spite of how chronic his addictions were, Joe first found recovery in Adult Child self-help groups, and from there he found his way to Alcoholics Anonymous.

JOE:

"I was bankrupt. I was worse than zero in every area of my life, working just enough to scrape by, when my daughter called me one day. She had shared many times how alike she thought we were, how we both felt alienated, how no one understood us, how we knew that we were okay somehow, deep inside, but that something was screwed up.

"That day she had been to counseling, and she said, 'I finally found out what our problem is.' Then she began to tell me about her

counseling and the Adult Child Twelve Step program. She brought me the literature, and I identified with it immediately. I know that I had found the answer. I'd always asked, 'What's the matter with me?' My first Adult Child self-help group meeting was like a white light experience. Through the ACOA literature and meetings I began to realize what was the matter with me. I had a feeling of intense gratitude, of finally knowing that I'd identified the problem, and that I'd found the solution."

Joe said it was in ACOA that he discovered he didn't want to drink anymore. He didn't believe he was alcoholic, but he began to attend AA meetings regularly to help him not drink.

"Finally, after going to AA meetings for three months, I had heard enough people talk about their lives that one night it hit me. I was one of them! I began to work the program, and I was very content for six months until I hit my sober bottom. I couldn't function sober. I couldn't face life without medication. But I also knew that was no longer an option, that it wouldn't work.

"One night driving home, I stopped at a red light. I was crying, and then I heard this little voice — my inner guide, my Higher Power — say, 'Joe, you can recover or die. You can work the Twelve Steps or die. Those are your only two choices.'

"I had reached that point, the real bottom. My only options were recover or die. I was out of bullshit. I was out of delays and fixes. I had to work the Twelve Steps or die. And I knew that. I called people that night, and I got sponsors, and I began to work the Twelve steps in both AA and ACOA.

"I am three years past that point now, and I've had some very rough times. It's a roller coaster, and I've hit some very hard bottoms. But now I'm seeing that they get farther and farther apart, and less and less intense."

Joe's Alcoholic/Addict and Adult Child Issues:

"I have needed both AA and ACOA in my life. My AA program has helped me to stay sober, to not drink and use. And it has also taught me a great deal about living life on life's terms.

"My ACOA program has really taught me to break out of the patterns of my past. I've been astounded when I've identified these hurtful patterns — seeing how that happened then affects what happens now. This has given me the courage to change these patterns: my compulsive spending; my overeating; my self-destructive, self-defeating, suicidal behavior; my sexual obsessions; my workaholism; my pursuit of esteem through accomplishments; and my terror of abandonment. So much of this has come from listening to other people and their stories. I share, and I listen. Other people have helped me tremendously.

"For the most part, I've lived alone during recovery. I had a relationship in which I chose a partner who wasn't able to be there for me emotionally. For the first time I was able to move out of the relationship without falling into a suicidal, life-threatening depression."

In the past Joe would have experienced suicidal thoughts and depression with such a separation. Recovery from Adult Child issues of abandonment becomes evident when we can feel the pain of loss but not toss out all that is positive in our lives because one aspect hurts.

"My depression is almost nonexistent today. And I've made major progress in all of my chemical and nonchemical addictions. I'm clean and sober chemically. Nonchemically I'm much better in my workaholism, my terror of abandonment, and my compulsive spending. I still isolate myself at times. But I'm getting to feel better around groups of people, even though I still feel awkward occasionally. I'm certainly not perfect. But I'm on the right path, and I feel that things are getting better every day."

As people recover from chemical dependency, they often uncover other addictive patterns. It is unrealistic to expect to resolve all of these issues quickly. Patience is a virtue that needs to be developed. What one has to do it is to acknowledge the little steps we take in the process.

"Often I have to look back at what I was like a month ago or six months ago or two years ago to realize how far I've come. Today I want everyone to know that I am happy. When I was in denial, I never once dreamed that I could ever be happy. When I was drinking, I'd forsaken all hope of ever being happy. But today I am. I'm happy even when external circumstances are not good. Basically I'm happy if I work my program and use my tools.

"I've learned to be my own loving parent. One of the major things I learned in my ACOA program was to get off my own case, to stop beating myself up verbally, to stop second-guessing, criticizing, and fault finding. I've learned to stop telling myself that I'll never be good enough, never be right. I've learned to tell myself that I'm okay. I know I'm going to make a lot of errors — errors are part of being human. I've had a lot to learn about just giving myself a break."

In his recovery Joe has learned a great deal about forgiveness and self-love.

"My feelings about my parents have rolled-coastered in my recovery years from intense hatred to an intense compulsion to rescue them. My dad has recently died. I will probably always wonder what he thought of me. Prior to his death I used the detachment I learned about in Al-Anon. I learned how to be there for my parents without hurting myself. I have also forgiven and released, and I think our relationship today is as good as it will ever get, and that's okay."

Joe has discovered what is essential to many recovering alcoholics/addicts, a way to allow a Higher Power to be incorporated into his life.

"The bottom line of my recovery is the concept that only God fills up the empty hole inside. I've tried to use everything else to fill it up, but it was never enough. I kept wondering what was missing, what was wrong. All my chemical and nonchemical dependencies were symptoms of the one disorder — my separation from a Higher Power.

I had the insane belief that I knew better than God how to create myself and how to run and manage my own life. Today I almost always find that if things aren't going well, it means I've been trying to run my own life again, that I've been trying to get my own agenda in, and that I haven't been asking to know God's will for my life.

"The **Course in Miracles** *has been another significant factor in facilitating my spiritual path. Through prayer and meditation I've been able to hear this inner voice better and better, and I've learned to trust it even further, and to use it as a daily guide. It's very important for me to stay in the here and now, one day at a time, and not try to see how everything fits into a pattern or plan for ten years down the line.*

"I'm very grateful to AA, ACOA, and the **Course in Miracles** *for bringing me back to the concept of a Higher Power. I find the knowledge that I can turn my life over to God very comforting."*

PROFILES FOR RECOVERY

In this book we have discussed the stories of five chemically dependent people who have chosen to explore their Adult Child issues. Each individual has traveled a unique path to the integration of a sobriety program with ACOA work.

Dennis, at the age of thirty-two, has been sober the longest — ten years — as he begins his Adult Child work. He could not have begun it much earlier, as the concept and resources for Adult Child recovery have only been available within the last ten years. Also, most people beginning their Adult Child work are in their thirties and forties. It often takes time in adult life for these issues to escalate to the level where an Adult Child feels it necessary to seek recovery resources. Although Dennis is young, the fact that he had been a part of a Twelve Step program facilitated his ability to recognize problems earlier than other Adult Children and to seek resources. He was well entrenched in his recovery from addiction when he began his Adult Child recovery.

Bob and Margaret are clear that their Adult Child issues interfere with their ability to use their AA recovery program. It was necessary for them to work on these issues to prevent relapse.

Although Bob was in a self-help program, he was not able to stay abstinent. His ACOA issues repeatedly interfered with his sobriety, and he would drink. But once he sought professional help for his Adult Child issues, his alcoholism was soon recognized as the immediate issue of importance. Bob entered an alcoholism-treatment program, and his focus, in early sobriety, was directed at his primary goal of abstinence. But the key to understanding his addiction lay in finally dealing with childhood issues around his alcoholic family. Only after he had begun this work was he able to accept his own alcoholism and his need to achieve and maintain sobriety.

When Margaret was a few years sober, she began rationalizing the use of Valium as a response to her problems with daily living. However, before she started to use, she was directed to an ACOA program, and at last her day-to-day problems began to resolve themselves.

Lisa may have had more time before her Adult Child issues smacked into her recovery process, but grief at the death of her teenage son, when she was only a year sober, put her in touch with family-of-origin issues that could no longer be denied or ignored.

Joe is one of the small but growing percentage of people who seek help for ACOA issues first and in doing so recognize their own alcoholism and get help for it.

No matter which profile one identifies with, it is my strong belief that Adult Child issues will in time deeply affect the quality of a person's sobriety. Exploring one's double identity as an Adult Child and addict can be an extremely fruitful source for self-examination and long-term recovery.

Alcohol/Addict Teenagers And COA Recovery

This material has been directed toward the Adult Child who is chemically dependent — not to the chemically dependent teenager. But it is my belief that these young people also have two identities. However, while I believe it is both possible and more appropriate for Adult Child alcoholics/addicts to separate their issues, I find neither to be true for the COA teenager. The older teens — seventeen, eighteen, nineteen year olds — may be able to deal with these issues separately, particularly if they do not live at home. But while younger teens, and those at home, need first and foremost to understand the need for total abstinence, it is crucial for them to work on COA issues simultaneously. They need a place to share their feelings about their family life. They need adults outside the home to provide structure and places where they can be involved in age-appropriate activities.

They need to learn the traditional Al-Anon principles of how to live in their families while also taking the best care of themselves.

Recovery Resources

There is no one right way to receive help. There is no one way to experience recovery. However, given the nature of the disease of chemical dependency, I feel it becomes one's primary identity. Being an Adult Child, then, is one's secondary identity. It is my bias that one cannot fully address one's Adult Child issues if one is not clean and sober. Practicing chemically dependent people are not capable of being honest with themselves or anyone else. They think delusionally.

The most likely resources for recovery lie in two areas. First the self-help groups: Alcoholics Anonymous, Cocaine Anonymous, Narcotics Anonymous. More people have received help through these Twelve Step programs than any other resource. Twelve Step self-help groups are free of charge and widespread throughout the world.

Second, there are the chemical dependency treatment programs. These are professionally staffed and structured programs that may be outpatient or inpatient. Although there are inpatient services that offer a detoxification program, usually both inpatient and outpatient services offer individual and group therapy resources. Available resources and costs vary. Local councils on alcoholism and information and referral sources are listed in Yellow Pages.

People can and do recover through other resources as well — for example, through their church, spiritual therapy, and other kinds of self-help support groups. But for the majority of chemically dependent people, the answers tend to be found in the combination of Twelve Step self-help groups and professional treatment.

Resources for working on Adult Child issues include individual and group psychotherapy as well as such Twelve Step programs as the Adult Children of Alcoholics and Co-dependency Anonymous self-help groups. Traditional Al-Anon meetings have always been and continue to be another resource for Adult Children. People who have double-duty issues or are dual-identity may find it safer to begin recovery with a helping professional. But even where this is true, it also helps to be open to the transition of using self-help groups as well.

Special Challenge Of Support

One of the difficulties recovering alcoholics and addicts often encounter in pursuing their Adult Child work is a lack of support from other recovering alcoholic/addicts.

It is difficult for people who have found a path that has produced miracles in their lives to be open to another approach, particularly one that touches so closely on areas where they are extremely vulnerable. They are often critical of others as a defense. As chemically dependent parents, they are vulnerable about the way their addictions have affected their own children and, again, as a defense against their own pain, are critical of others wanting to do Adult Child work.

When this occurs, it is important to remember that you are getting feedback from individual personalities within a recovery program. It is not the program itself that is being critical. Nowhere in the writings of Alcoholics Anonymous and Al-Anon does it say that one should continue to minimize, discount, or deny the pain of one's past. Above all, these are programs that recommend honesty as a basis for recovery; these are programs that teach self-responsibility.

Adult Child recovery means taking responsibility for oneself today as an adult. To do that, people have to explore their childhood years, speak the truth of their experiences, reframe hurtful internalized beliefs, and learn skills that they didn't have an opportunity to learn as children. Adult Child recovery is not meant to replace addiction recovery. It is meant to enhance every part of who one is.

Although people approach these issues from different directions, it is clear that when one is both an Adult Child and chemically dependent, one has two identities. The issues that affect both of these identities must be addressed if recovery is to be ongoing.

"My recovery has taught me that I am not my father. I am different. I am thirty-seven; he is sixty-two. I am recovering; he is not. He brought his family full term into their Adult child issues; I am doing what I can to break the cycle for my family in my lifetime."

Adult Child/Recovering alcoholic

APPENDIX

THE ORIGINAL LAUNDRY LIST FOR ADULT CHILDREN OF ALCOHOLICS

The Problem

The Characteristics we seem to have in common due to our being brought up in an alcoholic household:

A. We became isolated and afraid of people and authority figures.

B. We became approval seekers and lost our identity in the process.

C. We are frightened by angry people and any personal criticism.

D. We either become alcoholics, marry them, or both, or find another compulsive personality such as a workaholic to fulfill our sick abandonment needs.

E. We live life from the viewpoint of victims and are attracted by that weakness in our lives and friendship relationships.

F. We have an overdeveloped sense of responsibility and it is easier for us to be concerned with others rather than ourselves; this enables us not too look too closely at our own faults, etc.

G. We get guilt feelings when we stand up for ourselves instead of giving in to others.

H. We become addicted to excitement.

I. We confuse love and pity and tend to "love" people we can "pity" and "rescue."

J. We have stuffed our feelings from our traumatic childhoods and have lost the ability to feel or express our feelings because it hurts so much. (Denial)

K. We judge ourselves harshly and have a very low sense of self-esteem.

L. We are dependent personalities who are terrified of abandonment and will do anything to hold on to a relationship in order not to experience painful abandonment feelings which we received from living with sick people who were never there emotionally for us.

M. Alcoholism is a family disease and we became para-alcoholics and took on the characteristics of that disease even though we did not pick up the drink.

N. Para-alcoholics are reactors rather than actors.

The Solution

By attending Adult Children of Alcoholics meetings on a regular basis, we learn that we can live our lives in a more meaningful manner; we learn to change our attitudes and old patterns of behavior and habits, to find serenity, even happiness.

A. Alcoholism is a three-fold disease; mental, physical, and spiritual. Our parents are victims of this disease which either ends in death or insanity. This is the beginning of the gift of forgiveness.

B. We learn to put the focus on ourselves and to be good to ourselves.

C. We learn to detach with love; tough love.

D. We use the slogans: LET GO, LET GOD; EASY DOES IT; ONE DAY AT A TIME, etc.

E. We learn to feel our feelings, to accept and express them, and to build our self-esteem.

F. Through working the steps, we learn to accept the disease and to realize that our lives have become unmanageable and that we are powerless over the disease and that alcoholic. As we become willing to admit our defects and our sick thinking, we are able to change our attitudes and our reactions into actions. By working the program daily, admitting that we are powerless; we come to believe eventually in the spirituality of the program — that there is a solution other than ourselves, a Higher Power, God as we understand Him/She or by sharing our experiences, relating to others, welcoming newcomers, serving our group, we build our self-esteem.

PROGRESSION CHART
Alcohol Addiction

Read from left to right

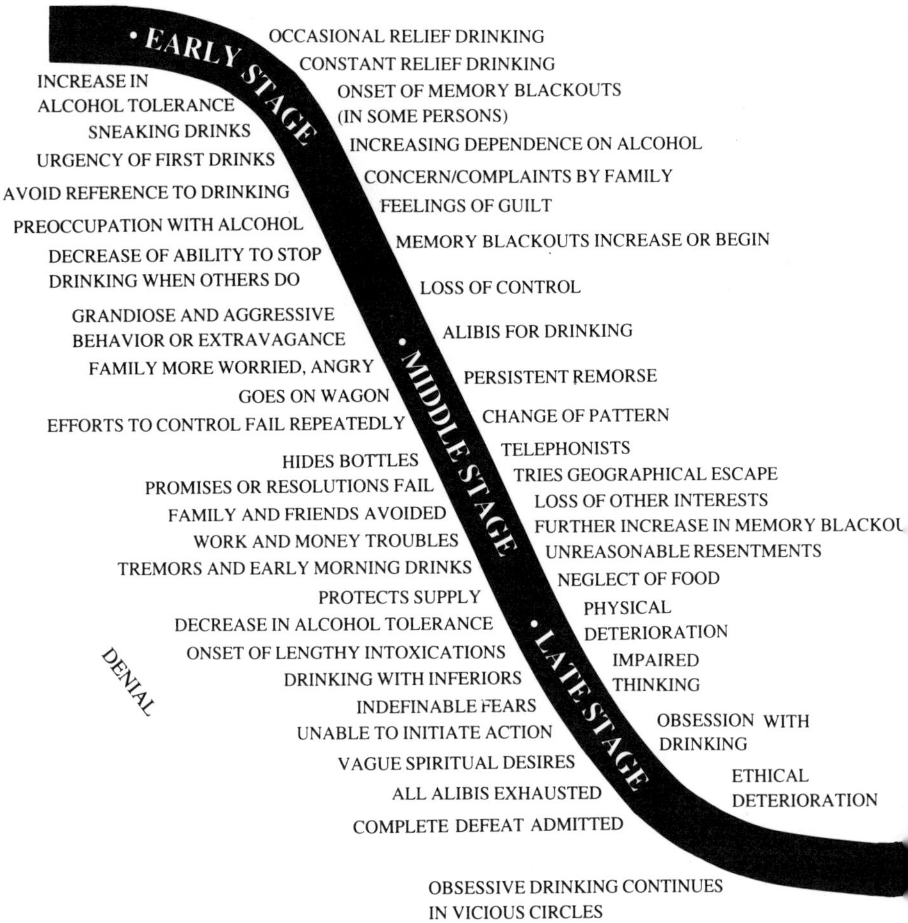

THE ROAD TO RECOVERY

— Modified form M.M. Glatt

DO YOU HAVE THE DISEASE OF ALCOHOLISM?

When considering the possibility of alcoholism, please consider two things: First, the nature of the disease is to trick its victims into believing they can control their drinking. Second, making an effort to control one's drinking is, by itself, a sign of alcoholism. People who don't have an alcohol problem don't think twice about how much they drink. They set a limit and stick to it. If your drinking causes problems in any area of your life with your family, at work, in social settings, emotionally or physically, financially, or with the law, it's worth finding out more about this disease.

Alcoholism strikes one out of every ten people who drink. Not everyone has the physiological makeup to become alcoholic, but anyone who drinks could be at risk. Alcoholism doesn't discriminate. It affects people of all ethnic backgrounds, professions, and economic levels. It is not known precisely what causes this disease, but drinking is clearly a prerequisite. Therefore everyone who drinks should periodically evaluate their drinking patterns and behavior. This test, reproduced with permission of the National Council on Alcoholism, Inc. (NCA), will help you to determine whether or not you have symptoms of the disease. Answer the questions honestly, with a simple yes or no.

	Yes	No
1. Do you occasionally drink heavily after a disappointment, a quarrel, or when the boss gives you a hard time?	___	___
2. When you have trouble or feel under pressure, do you always drink more heavily than usual?	___	___

	Yes	No
3. Have you noticed that you are able to handle more alcohol than you did when you were first drinking?	___	___
4. Did you ever wake up on the *"morning after"* and discover that you could not remember part of the evening before, even though your friends tell you that you did not *"pass out"*?	___	___
5. When drinking with other people, do you try to have a few extra drinks when others will not know it?	___	___
6. Are there certain occasions when you feel uncomfortable if alcohol is not available?	___	___
7. Have you recently noticed that when you begin drinking you are in more of a hurry to get the first drink than you used to be?	___	___
8. Do you sometimes feel a little guilty about your drinking?	___	___
9. Are you secretly irritated when your family or friends discuss your drinking?	___	___
10. Have you recently noticed an increase in the frequency of your memory *"blackouts"*?	___	___
11. Do you often find that you wish to continue drinking after your friends say they have had enough?	___	___
12. Do you usually have a reason for the occasions when you drink heavily?	___	___
13. When you are sober, do you often regret things you have done or said while you were drinking?	___	___
14. Have you tried switching brands or following different plans for controlling your drinking?	___	___

	Yes	No
15. Have you often failed to keep the promises you have made to yourself about controlling or cutting down on your drinking?	___	___
16. Have you ever tried to control your drinking by making a change in jobs or moving to a new location?	___	___
17. Do you try to avoid family or close friends while you are drinking?	___	___
18. Are you having an increasing number of financial and work problems?	___	___
19. Do more people seem to be treating you unfairly without good reason?	___	___
20. Do you eat very little or irregularly when you are drinking?	___	___
21. Do you sometimes have the *"shakes"* in the morning and find that it helps to have a little drink?	___	___
22. Have you recently noticed that you cannot drink as much as you once did?	___	___
23. Do you sometimes stay drunk for several days at a time?	___	___
24. Do you sometimes feel very depressed and wonder whether life is worth living?	___	___
25. Sometimes after periods of drinking, do you see or hear things that are not there?	___	___
26. Do you get terribly frightened after you have been drinking heavily?	___	___

Any "*yes*" answer indicated a probable symptom of alcoholism. "*Yes*" answers to several of the questions indicate the following stages of alcoholism:

Questions 1 to 8: Early stage.
Questions 9 to 21: Middle stage.
Questions 22 to 26: Beginning of final stage.

Volunteers at local affiliate offices of NCA can provide further information to help you assess whether or not you have a drinking problem. They can also refer you to services and treatment programs in your area. Check the phone book under "Alcohol" or call **1-800-NCA-CALL** (1-800-622-2255) for the number of your community's NCA affiliate.

NOTES

1 Black C., Bucky S., Padilla S. 1986. *The interpersonal emotional consequences of being an Adult Child of an Alcoholic.* Journal of International Addictions 21,213, 232
2 Hrubec, A., & Omenn, G.S. 1981. *Evidence of genetic predisposition to alcoholic cirrhosis and psychois:* Twin concordances for alcoholism and its biological end points by zygosity among male veterans. Alcoholism: Clinical and experimental Research, 5, 207 - 215.
3 Bohman, M. 1978. *Archives of General Psychiatry,* 35, 269 - 276.
Bohman, M., Sigvardsson, S., & Cloninger, R. 1981. *Archives of General Psychiatry,* 38, 965 - 969.
Goodwin, D.W. 1985. *Archives of General Psychiatry,* 34, 751 - 755.
4 Kern, J.C., Hassett, C.A. & Collipp, P.J. 1981. *Journal of Psychiatric Treatment and Evaluation,* 3, 169 - 173.
5 Schuckit, M.A., & Rayses, V. 1979. *Science* 203, 54 - 55.
6 Schuckit, M.A. 1984. *Journal of Studies on Alcohol,* 45, 334 - 338. Archives of General Psychiatry, 41, 879 - 884.

Books by Claudia Black

My Dad Loves Me, My Dad Has A Disease

It Will Never Happen To Me

Repeat After Me

It's Never Too Late To Have A Happy Childhood

Double Duty — Gay—Lesbian

Double Duty — Chemically Dependent

Double Duty — Food Addiction

Double Duty — Sexual Abuse

A complete catalogue of MAC products, including videotapes, note cards and related material, can be obtained free of charge from:

MAC PUBLISHING
a division of Claudja, inc.
5005 East 39th Avenue
Denver, CO 80207
(303) 331-0148 • Fax (303) 331-0212